Revisiting the Welfare State

ROBERT M. PAGE

Open University Press

Open University Press
McGraw-Hill Education
McGraw-Hill House
Shoppenhangers Road
Maidenhead
Berkshire
England
SL6 2QL

email: enquiries@openup.co.uk
world wide web: www.openup.co.uk

and Two Penn Plaza, New York, NY 10121-2289, USA

First published 2007

A catalogue record of this book is available from the British Library

ISBN13: 978 0 335 21317 7 (pb)   978 0 335 21318 4 (hb)
ISBN10: 0 335 21317 0 (pb)   0 335 21318 9 (hb)

Library of Congress Cataloging-in-Publication Data
CIP data has been applied for

Typeset by RefineCatch Ltd, Bungay, Suffolk
Printed in Poland EU by Pozkal
www.polskabook.pl

The McGraw·Hill Companies

Revisiting the Welfare State

INTRODUCING SOCIAL POLICY SERIES
Series Editor: David Gladstone

Published titles

For Jane with love

Contents

Series editor's foreword

Welcome to the eighth volume in the Introducing Social Policy series. The series itself is designed to provide a range of well informed texts on a variety of topics that fall within the ambit of social policy studies.

Although primarily designed with undergraduate social policy students in mind, it is hoped that the series – and individual titles within it – will have a wider appeal to students in other social science disciplines and to those engaged on professional and post-qualifying courses in health care and social welfare.

The aim throughout the planning of the series has been to produce a series of texts that both reflect and contribute to contemporary thinking and scholarship, and which present their discussion in a readable and easily accessible format.

The fifth of July 2008 marks the 60th anniversary of the implementation of the National Health Service and the schemes of National Insurance and Assistance designed to provide 'cradle to grave' financial security to the British population. It was described by Clement Attlee, the then Labour Prime Minister as 'a day which makes history'. In the context of post-war austerity that was no exaggerated boast: for, along with the 1944 Education Act, Town and Country Planning legislation and a commitment to full employment, it was the culmination of Britain's 'classic' welfare state, a New Deal for the British people, a transformation from warfare to welfare. The intervening sixty years have seen the growing importance of welfare issues in domestic politics, as well as a transformation in the supply of welfare services. If the transition in the 1940s was from warfare to welfare, the first decade of the twenty-first century has witnessed another New Deal: from welfare to workfare.

This is but the outline of the welfare story which Robert Page tells so graphically in this book. Drawing on a wide range of sources, he not only provides a well-informed narrative of welfare state change, but also of the dynamics of 'the five giants': the core services that provide the political commitment to welfare. Furthermore, he acts as an informed and stimulating guide to some of the central debates in the history of Britain's welfare experience over the past sixty years: the role of the Second World War in the creation of a more generous and fairer society; the alleged consensus between Conservative and Labour parties in government in the years between 1951 and 1979; and the continuities between the radical Conservatism of Thatcher and Major and their New Labour successors in office. Market practices, consumerism and diversity may, as Page tantalizingly suggests, betoken an emerging cross-party concordat on welfare, present and future. But to those of us who have lived through this period, they also suggest a significant shift away from the transformative vision of Attlee's Appointed Day.

What better time, then, to revisit Britain's Welfare State.

David Gladstone
University of Bristol

Acknowledgements

It has been my immense good fortune and delight to have had a series editor such as David Gladstone. He has been supportive throughout. It is to his immense credit that he has remained so courteous and patient during the gestation period of this book, which like a previous title in this series, Alan Deacon's *Perspectives on Welfare* has taken an 'unconscionable time to write'.

I owe an immense debt to Jane Wilton who might have had second thoughts about accepting a proposal of marriage if she knew it was likely to involve reading successive draft chapters of a social policy text in her 'spare' time. Her fine eye for detail, and her constructive and perceptive suggestions for improving this book have been invaluable.

I would also like to take this opportunity to record my thanks to those who have been particular supportive of my academic endeavours over the years – Vic George, John Baldock, Don Cooper, Baron Duckham, Bill Silburn, John Ferris, Gill Pascall, Bob Pinker, Alan Deacon, Jane Aldgate, Kwame Owusu Bempah and Michael Sullivan.

List of abbreviations

ABCA	Army Bureau of Current Affairs
ALMO	arm's length management organization
ARP	Air Raid Precautions service
BBC	British Broadcasting Corporation
BMA	British Medical Association
CPC	Conservative Political Centre
CSJ	Commission on Social Justice
DfEE	Department for Education and Employment
GCSE	General Certificate of Secondary Education
GM	grant-maintained
GPs	General Practitioners
HMI	Her Majesty's Inspectorate
IEA	Institute of Economic Affairs
IMF	International Monetary Fund
LEA	local education authority
LLP	London Labour Party
LMS	local management of schools
MUD	moral underclass discourse
NALT	National Association of Labour Teachers
NHS	National Health Service
NICE	National Institute for Clinical Excellence
OFSTED	Office for Standards in Education
ONG	One Nation Group
PEP	Political and Economic Planning
QUANGO	QUasi-Autonomous Non-Governmental Organization
RED	redistributionist discourse
SB	Supplementary Benefit
SERPS	State earnings-related pension scheme
SID	social integrationist discourse
VAT	Value Added Tax

Introduction

The development of the British welfare state has been the subject of a number of scholarly publications. The pioneering work of Maurice Bruce (1961), Bentley Gilbert (1970) and Derek Fraser (1973) has been complemented by texts devoted to the period before the Second World War such as J.D. Hay (1983), and Bernard Harris (2004), as well as others that focus on developments since 1945 (Sullivan 1992; Hill 1993; Deakin 1994; Gladstone 1999; Timmins 2001; Lowe 2005; Glennerster 2007).

Although it is widely acknowledged that the study of social policy can be enriched by an appreciation of its historical and political contexts, there remains a sense in which such material is more often regarded as a preparation for the study of contemporary social policy, rather than an integral part of the subject itself. As Gladstone (2003) notes, 'those who study social policy are often more concerned with the present and the future than with the past' (p. 25). One of the reasons why there are likely to be differing opinions over the centrality or otherwise of political history for the study of welfare is that the discipline of social policy itself has a more 'porous' identity than many allied subjects, such as sociology or economics. The fact that a number of university departments of social policy have been established (and disestablished) over the past 40 years or so, and that a membership organization (the Social Policy Association) has been functioning since 1967 has done little to solidify the key constituent components of the subject or its boundaries. There are those, for example, who contend that the subject should, in keeping with its previous incarnation as social administration (see Mishra 1977), remain 'problem' focused with an emphasis on empirical investigation that can give rise to policy initiatives that 'improve' the functioning of society and human well being. Others, in contrast, believe that the study of social policy should use the insights derived from neighbouring subjects to develop more 'sophisticated' theoretical perspectives concerning the role and purpose of social policy in modern societies. In many ways it could be argued that a key strength of the academic study of social policy is that it defies easy classification. Diversity of this kind can, though, make it more difficult to build up collective strength and purpose.

This book starts from the premise that the student of social policy can gain a deeper understanding of the welfare state by studying political and historical accounts of the welfare state, party manifestos and policy documents, and political memoirs. It can be argued that a focus of this kind gives undue prominence to the influence of parties and key actors. Our understanding of social policy will, however, be much the poorer if these aspects of social policy are downplayed or ignored.

A number of key historical and political issues relating to the development of the British welfare state since 1940 are examined in this volume. The intention is not to challenge or disprove previous theories or explanations, but rather to engage with them. It is hoped that there will be many other such reappraisals of the post-1940 welfare state.

Each of the five main chapters in the book is devoted to particular themes associated with the British welfare state since 1940. Chapter One revisits the issue of the impact of the Second World War on civilian behaviour and attitudes. Did the war act as a catalyst for major economic and social change? Did a consensus emerge between Conservative and Labour members of Churchill's coalition wartime government between 1940 and 1945 about the welfare state? In terms of the first of these themes, evidence of the 'progressive' impact of war, such as increased selflessness, the permeation of a 'never again' attitude amongst the public, the media, the Church and in official publications, such as the Beveridge Report is examined. Positive information of this kind is contrasted with examples of disunity on the Home Front, such as crime, the harsh treatment of aliens, anti-Semitism, strikes, absenteeism and unequal civilian 'sacrifices'. On balance, it is concluded that the 'Titmuss thesis', which suggests that the war had a 'progressive' impact on the conduct and attitudes of the British public, remains persuasive. The suggestion that a welfare consensus emerged between Conservative and Labour members of the coalition government seems harder to substantiate. Although agreement was reached in a number of policy areas, there remained, as the 1945 General Election campaign confirmed, fundamental and irreconcilable differences between the two main parties over the role and purpose of the welfare state.

The democratic socialist welfare strategy of the post-war Attlee governments from 1945 to 1951 is revisited in Chapter Two. Despite adverse economic circumstances, the Labour Party set about creating a welfare state that would bring a greater level of security and enhanced opportunities for all citizens. The various strengths and weaknesses of Labour's initiatives in the areas of social security, health, education and housing are reviewed. Given the austere climate in which Labour was operating it is not surprising to find that Labour's welfare initiatives fell short of the highest democratic socialist standards. They did, however, represent a significant step forward. Crucially, Labour's welfare policies formed part of a wider desire to create a socialist commonwealth. This broader goal proved more problematic as Labour was uncertain about what type of economy it wanted to create and what other institutional changes would be necessary to bring about a socialist society. The social conservatism of the Party leadership is highlighted as problematic in this regard. Moreover, it is suggested that Labour may have over-estimated the public's appetite for socialism. The 'fair shares' ethos that emerged during the war did not necessarily carry over into peacetime. By the time Labour left office in 1951 there were conflicting views within the Party about the way ahead.

Chapter Three revisits the thorny issue of whether a welfare consensus developed between Labour and the Conservatives in the period from 1951 and 1979. Adopting Pimlott's (1988) thesis that a consensus requires an ideological agreement, the respective approaches of the two parties towards the welfare state are considered. It is argued that the Conservatives adopted a more favourable approach towards the welfare state during the period from 1945 to 1964 when modern conservatism was in the ascendancy. The One Nation Group, which had been established in 1950, was instrumental in developing a more positive accord with the welfare state which did not pose a threat to traditional Conservative values such as 'sound' money, low taxation, self-reliance and the voluntary ethic. Importantly, this new thinking did not signal an ideological conversion to Labour's egalitarian strategy. Instead, a distinctive Conservative approach to the welfare state with an emphasis on minimum standards and greater selectivity was set down.

After a period of consolidation, Labour turned to a revisionist form of democratic socialism, based on many of the ideas put forward in Anthony Crosland's (1956) seminal text *The Future of Socialism*. Labour remained committed to the establishment of a more equal society but now believed that extensive nationalization was not required to ensure that 'modern' capitalism operated in ways that maximized the public interest. Moreover, the welfare state came to be seen as a more appropriate mechanism for bringing about an egalitarian society than further measures of income redistribution. Labour's insistence that its welfare strategy was dependent on sustained economic growth proved problematic. In an era of economic turbulence and low growth it was difficult to make any sustained progress in social policy. Indeed, by the late 1960s and 1970s it was even being suggested that the welfare state might be having a negative, rather than positive, effect on the economy and the wider society.

Although there were points of similarity between the Conservatives and Labour in relation to social policy in the period from 1951 to 1979, it is concluded that it is difficult to sustain the proposition that a welfare consensus emerged during this period. Significant ideological differences between the parties over the welfare state remained.

The Conservative welfare 'revolution' that was said to have occurred between 1979 and 1997 is revisited in Chapter Four. Consecutive defeats in the General Elections of 1974 led to growing interest in neo-liberal ideas within the Party. These ideas came to the fore following the election of Margaret Thatcher as the party's leader in 1975. Returning to government on a neo-liberal platform in 1979, Thatcher sought to reverse Britain's reputation as the 'sick man of Europe' by curbing inflation, lowering taxes, controlling the trade unions, reducing public expenditure and creating a more entrepreneurial ethos in society. Although the economic and social costs of what could be described as 'confrontational' Conservatism were high, Thatcher succeeded in achieving many of her objectives. It is questionable, though, whether Thatcher presided over a welfare revolution. While Thatcher and many of her leading cabinet ministers were committed in principle to rolling back the welfare state, the political and economic costs of such a revolutionary strategy were judged too high. Accordingly, radical reform of the welfare state, rather than revolution, became the order of the day.

Although John Major distanced himself from some of the more unpopular policies of his predecessor such as the Poll Tax and was more sympathetic to the ideals of a welfare state, he did not change direction to any substantial extent. Consolidation proved to be his watchword. The final part of this chapter is devoted to an assessment of whether Thatcher and Major were welfare 'revolutionaries'.

It could be argued that it is premature to 'revisit' New Labour when they are still in office. However, the fact that they have had such a dramatic effect on the political landscape since abandoning their Party's traditional revisionist democratic socialist approach to welfare, provides a strong reason for reviewing their approach in Chapter Five of this volume. Unlike previous post-1945 Labour governments, New Labour has adopted a much more favourable approach towards the market, and has been less concerned about rising income and wealth inequalities, which they believe have irreversible 'global', rather than 'national' causes. New Labour has pursued what they have termed a 'third way' or 'modern social democratic' approach towards the welfare state and society. They believe that a modern welfare state must be pro-active, rather than passive, encourage a diverse range of providers, be 'customer' orientated, and extend opportunities to all. Following an examination of key elements of the welfare strategy of the Blair administrations, it is concluded that New Labour has striven to put its principles into effect, albeit with varying levels of success. It is acknowledged that New Labour's perception of a 'progressive' welfare policy will not find favour with traditional Labour supporters who believe that the party has abandoned its commitment to equality, universalism and public provision of services. The chapter concludes by suggesting that New Labour's accommodation with some of the tenets of traditional Conservatism, coupled with David Cameron's professed desire to tackle relative poverty and increase opportunities for the most disadvantaged, may finally give rise to the first ideological welfare consensus.

Further reading

There are some excellent accounts of the development of the British welfare state since the Second World War. Few would dispute that the texts by Timmins (2001), Lowe (2005) and Glennerster (2007) deserve a place on the bookshelf of anyone interested in the contemporary history of the welfare state.

chapter

one

The impact of war on the 'Home' Front, the coalition government and the Welfare State

This chapter will examine two central issues relating to the impact of the Second World War on British society. First, attention will be focused on the question of whether the experience of war on the Home Front led to more 'progressive' social attitudes and a greater appetite for egalitarian forms of state intervention. Secondly, the approach to social policy adopted by Churchill's coalition government will be examined. Did Conservative and Labour members of the wartime coalition share a common understanding of the role and purpose of state intervention that could be described as a consensus, or was this merely a wartime accord that could not be sustained in the immediate post-war period?

The impact of the Second World War on social attitudes

After being out of power since 1931, the Labour Party recognized that 'total war' would provide a unique opportunity to convince the British people that Labour's interventionist approach to economic and social issues could lead to significant improvements in well-being. At the Party's Annual Conference in 1940, Attlee told the assembled delegates that 'the world that must emerge from this war must be a world attuned to our ideals' (quoted in Brooke 1992: 1). Labour's dramatic victory in the 1945 General Election suggests that nearly half of the adult population had indeed been persuaded that a Labour government would better serve their interests than a return to Conservative rule. To what extent then can it be said that wartime experiences were responsible for this change in Party allegiance? In one of the official wartime histories, Richard Titmuss (1950) came to the firm conclusion that the prospect of invasion, coupled with the impact and consequences of enemy bombing raids led to an upsurge in community spirit, less pronounced class distinctions and a desire for a more egalitarian society:

> The mood of the people changed, and in sympathetic response, values changed as well. If dangers were to be shared, then resources should also be shared . . . dramatic events on the home front served to reinforce the war-warmed impulse of people for a more generous society.
>
> (Titmuss 1950: 508)

Of course, it is difficult to arrive at a definitive conclusion concerning the way in which wartime experiences gave rise to public demands for economic and social change. However, there are a number of factors that appear to support what could be described as the 'progressive impact of war' thesis.

Increased selflessness

Many of those involved in the war on the Home Front have commented on the friendliness and camaraderie they experienced during the war. Gioya Steinke, a welfare adviser with the London County Council Rest Centre Service, recalls telling a 'perfect stranger' how she longed for a bath. The stranger 'handed me her keys, told me her address and said, "Go to the house tomorrow and have a bath and leave the keys under the mat. She said that if I could take my own soap and towel, she'd be pleased but if I couldn't, that was all right" ' (quoted in Levine 2006: 349).

According to Titmuss (1950), the government's voluntary evacuation scheme also demonstrated the selfless sentiments of the British public:

> For the authorities to impose – and to maintain for almost five years – a policy of billeting in private homes was a severe test of the better side of human nature. It was a formidable – to some an intolerable – burden for any government to place on a section of its people. A community less kindly, less self-controlled, less essentially Christian in behaviour, would not have acquiesced to the same extent and for such a long period of time as this one did.
>
> (p. 388)

The government's evacuation scheme alerted those in the countryside to the deprivation of large numbers of poverty stricken inner city children. Significant numbers of evacuee children arrived in shoddy clothing and 'shoes with cardboard soles' (Calder 1971: 44). Many were found to be suffering from head lice, scabies and other skin diseases. Standards of cleanliness amongst the evacuee children also proved to be a source of concern. Many children had come from overcrowded homes that lacked a bath or separate WC. In the face of such widespread deprivation many householders may have had cause to reflect on the broader structural causes of such deprivation. Equally, though, others might have been more inclined to look to individualistic explanations to explain the poor condition of the evacuees. As McNicol (1986) notes:

> When considering the long-term effects of the social debate on evacuation . . . we must recognise that, as well as helping to construct an ideological climate favourable to welfare legislation, it also boosted a conservative, behaviouristic analysis of poverty that viewed the root cause of the children's condition as family failure, poor parenting and general social inadequacy.
>
> (p. 24)

Citizens on the Home Front displayed selflessness in many other ways. There was a positive response to the appeal made to workers in May 1940 by the Minister of Supply, Herbert Morrison, to 'Go to it'. 'Many factories went over to seven-day working. Shifts of ten or twelve hours became routine in whole sectors of war industry. And, it should be noted, this was achieved without the Government needing to resort to coercive measures' (Mackay 2002: 61). In addition, there was an upsurge in voluntary activity, notably with the Air Raid Precautions service (ARP). According to Mackay:

> the phenomenon of unpaid volunteering throughout the six years of the war was one of its characteristic features and surely one of the most striking indicators of the robust state of civilian morale. Of the one and a half million civilians who made up ARP's 'fourth arm' of wardens, firefighters, rescue workers, ambulance drivers, medical staff, telephonists and messengers, no fewer than four-fifths were unpaid volunteers.
>
> (p. 132)

There were also countless daily examples of the 'Dunkirk' spirit. For example, Titmuss (1950) relates how workers on their way to Victoria Station, upon encountering Charity Service Organization staff struggling to deal with a consignment of food, blankets and clothing from the Canadian Red Cross in Blitz-torn London, immediately offered to help. 'The sight of Red Cross labels and the emotional stimulus of bombing broke down traditional dignities and liberated a spirit of helpfulness' (p. 262).

A 'never again' ethos

There is much evidence to suggest that the experience of war contributed to the creation of a 'never again' ethos amongst the British public. As Hennessy (1993) contends, this phrase 'captures the motivating impulse of the first half-dozen years after the war – never again would there be war; never again would the British people be housed in slums, living off a meagre diet thanks to low wages or no wages at all; never again would mass unemployment blight the lives of millions; never again would natural abilities remain dormant in the absence of educational stimulus' (p. 2).

A number of surveys and studies conducted by the polling organization Gallup, the Home Intelligence Division of the Ministry of Information (McLaine 1979) and Mass Observation (which had been established in 1936 by Charles Madge, Tom Harrison and Humphrey Jennings to gather information on public attitudes and behaviour – Harrison 1978) confirmed the emergence of a 'never again' ethos. According to a Home Intelligence Division report of 1942, for example, there was substantial civilian support for a new society characterized by full employment, better employee rights, a more equal distribution of income and educational reform (Mackay 2002: 230).

Wartime experiences also appeared to be 'radicalizing' those serving in the armed forces. Interestingly, the Army Bureau of Current Affairs (ABCA), established in 1941 to counteract boredom amongst service personnel, was seen as contributing to this attitudinal shift by providing coverage of political issues. An ABCA publication summarizing the Beveridge Report in 1942 led one outraged Conservative MP, Maurice Petherick, to write to Churchill's Parliamentary Private Secretary, Harvie-Watt, urging him to curb the activities of the Bureau. According to Petherick, a failure to act would lead to 'the creatures coming back all pansy-pink' (Addison 1992: 355). While the precise impact of ABCA activity is open to question (see Summerfield 1981), it did appear to engender a greater degree of critical awareness about social issues amongst the Forces. Indeed, when a mock General Election was held in one of the 'Forces Parliaments' in Cairo in 1944, there was overwhelming support for the Labour Party (which attracted 119 votes), rather than the Conservatives, who polled just 17 votes (Mason and Thompson 1991: 57).

Voices for change

The case for social change was taken up by the media, film makers, the Church and, most famously in the Beveridge Report itself. Although both Churchill and the Ministry of Information were reluctant to enter into any debate concerning non-military 'war aims', they found it difficult to quell interest in this subject. A famous editorial written by E. H. Carr in *The Times*, for example, made a clarion call for the transformation of society:

> If we speak of democracy we do not mean a democracy which maintains the right to vote but forgets the right to work and the right to live.
> If we speak of freedom we do not mean a rugged individualism which excludes social organization and economic planning. If we speak of

equality we do not mean a political equality nullified by social and economic privilege.

(Carr, The Times, 1 July 1940)

Reconstruction was a major theme in the high circulation weekly magazine, *Picture Post*, which had become renowned as a 'popularizer of the views of intellectuals and progressive politicians' (Addison 1977: 152). In the edition of 4 January 1941, entitled *A Plan for Britain*, authors such as Thomas Balogh, A.D.K. Owen, Maxwell Fry, A.D. Lindsay, Julian Huxley and J.B. Priestley set out some of the political and social changes they deemed necessary in the areas of employment, social security, planning, education, health care and leisure. As the foreword to this edition made clear, 'Our plan for a new Britain is not something outside the war or something *after* the war. It is an essential part of our war aims. It is indeed, our most positive war aim. The new Britain is the country we are fighting for' (*Picture Post*, 10(1), 4 January 1941: 4). Not surprisingly, the sale of left-wing publications soared in this period. According to Addison (1977), by the end of the war nearly half of the national newspaper market had been captured by left-wing dailies compared with just 30% in 1930.

The British Broadcasting Corporation (BBC) caught the mood for change. In a number of radio 'postscripts' broadcast on Sunday evenings after the nine o'clock news between June and October 1940, J.B. Priestley gave full expression to 'never again' sympathies (Priestley 1940). Despite becoming 'Britain's first radio personality' with an estimated audience of some 30% of the population (Smith 2000: 47), Priestley nevertheless was, in the words of George Orwell, 'shoved off the air' after complaints from Conservative MPs about his socialist sympathies (Orwell, cited in Davidson 2001: 122; see also Addison 1977: 119). This sparked off 'a spate of newspaper articles and letters to editors, most of which were opposed to what they saw as the muzzling of a popular speaker who was asking questions that needed to be asked' (Mackay 2002: 227).

Film makers also took up the 'never again' theme (Mackay 2002). Three films made by John Baxter between 1941 and 1942, *Love on the Dole, The Common Touch* and *Let the People Sing*, highlighted the need for radical change in society. Similar sentiments could also be detected in government sponsored films such as the Boutling brothers' documentary *The Dawn Guard*, which focused on the activities of the Home Guard, as well as those of the legendary Humphrey Jennings (Jackson 2004). In a film entitled *A Diary for Timothy*, a record of the closing stages of the war is made in diary form for a newly born child, Timothy. In the closing sequence of the film, the narrator, Michael Redgrave (a leading actor of the period), asks Timothy whether he is going to allow 'greed for money or power' to oust 'decency from the world as they have in the past' or whether he will endeavour 'to make the world a different place'.

Other institutions promoted the case for change. Indeed, some such as the Fabian Society had been setting out agendas for change for many years before the war. As Mackay (2002) notes, 'By 1943 there were more than one hundred unofficial organizations studying and putting out ideas and proposals on different aspects of post-war reconstruction: land and town planning, industry and economics, agriculture, housing and public amenities, education, medicine and health' (p. 222).

The Church of England advanced the case for social change as well. A conference was held in Malvern in 1941 to consider the role that the Church could play in the reconstruction of society. In a subsequent letter to *The Times* published in 1942, the Archbishops of Canterbury, York and Westminster, and the Moderator of the Free Church called for an end to gross inequalities and unequal opportunities. The newly enthroned Archbishop of Canterbury, William Temple (who became known as the 'people's archbishop') returned to this theme in his influential Penguin publication, *Christianity and the Social Order*. In this book Temple (1942), a former member of the Labour Party, expanded on many of the themes raised at the Malvern conference, arguing that welfare reforms such as paid holidays and family allowances were fully in line with Anglican teaching (Lewis 1986; Kent 1992).

It was the publication of the Beveridge Report in 1942, however, that seemed to epitomize the 'never again' spirit in British society. Public interest in the report, the contents of which had been trailed in a series of articles and broadcasts in the weeks leading up to its official release (Harris 1997: 416), was confirmed by the forming of large queues at Her Majesty's Stationery Office in the Strand when the Report was published on 1 December. One Mass Observation respondent was overheard to remark:

> It's extraordinary the interest people are taking in it. When I went down to the stationery office to get it there were queues of people buying it & I was looking at it on the bus and the conductor said 'I suppose you haven't got a spare copy of that?'
>
> (Quoted in Jefferys 1994: 95)

Over 100,000 copies of the Report were sold within a month of publication and a 'special cheap edition was printed for circulation in the armed services' (Harris 1997: 415). While some more recent commentators such as George (1973) and Kincaid (1975) have questioned the accuracy of Beveridge's suggestion that his proposals for social security were revolutionary (cmd 6404 1942: 6), it is clear that the positive public response to the Report was based on a belief that this publication did indeed signal that the transformation of British society had begun in earnest. It was not the technical rigour of the Report, important though this was to assuage sceptics in Treasury circles and beyond, but rather the 'rich vein of Cromwellian and Bunyanesque prose' that struck a chord with a war weary public (Timmins

2001: 23). The benign white-haired knight setting forth to tackle the five giants of want, idleness, squalor, disease and ignorance had captured the public mood for a better tomorrow.

The 'never again' spirit was inevitably reflected in the sphere of party politics. As Mason and Thompson (1991) point out, 'All the political parties of the Left enjoyed substantial increases in membership during the war years. Membership of the Labour Party increased significantly from 2,663,000 in 1939 to 3,039,000 in 1945, and at a time when it had lost many members through population movements and conscription to the armed forces' (p. 56).

The absence of a wartime General Election coupled with an electoral truce (under which the mainstream parties in the coalition government agreed not to oppose any by-election candidate standing in a seat that their Party had held prior to the outbreak of war), makes it difficult to assess the strength of public support for social change at this time (Howard 2005). The wartime electoral success of a new, left wing party – Common Wealth – does, however, lend support to the view that public support for Labour would have increased during the war years.

Established in 1942, following the merger of J.B. Priestley's *1941 Committee* (whose supporters included David Astor, Victor Gollancz, Douglas Jay, François Lafitte and Richard Titmuss) and Sir Richard Acland's *Forward March* movement, Common Wealth pressed the case for the immediate adoption of a socialist war strategy following the fall of Tobruk in North Africa to the German army in 1941 (see Jefferys 1994). Following Allied success at El Alamein a year later, Common Wealth focused more sharply on 'civilian' issues, such as common ownership, enhanced forms of democracy including proportional representation and joint consultation in industry, and a greater morality in political life. Although committed to democratic means, Common Wealth adopted a more radical policy agenda than the Labour Party (Calder 1971).

In seeking to create a 'classless New Jerusalem' (p. 632), Common Wealth proved particularly appealing to the 'Utopian middle class' (Brooke 1992: 69). Certainly, most of its members could be described as middle class and its three hundred or so branches 'tended to be found in the wealthy suburbs rather than the working class areas' (p. 633). Between February 1943 and April 1945 Common Wealth fielded candidates in eight by-elections winning three seats – Eddisbury (April 1943), Skipton (January 1944) and Chelmsford (April 1945). Common Wealth's success in the 'sleepy agricultural backwater' (Calder 1971: 635) of Eddisbury was particular noteworthy given that Labour had previously deemed the constituency unwinnable and, in consequence, had not contested the seat. Common Wealth also supported Charlie White who, having resigned from the Labour Party to stand as an independent Labour candidate, succeeded in defeating Lord Hartington in the infamous Derbyshire West by-election of February 1944 (pp. 637–9).

Disunity on the Home Front

Although there are numerous examples of the ways in which the war engendered more progressive social attitudes and selfless behaviour on the Home Front, it is important not to overlook contrary evidence. Four forms of anti-social behaviour will be considered, crime, the treatment of aliens and anti-Semitism, strikes and absenteeism and 'unequal' sacrifices.

Crime

Crime increased markedly during the war. Indictable crimes reported to the police in England and Wales had risen by 21% in the 5-year period prior to 1939. Between 1939 and 1945 this rate increased to 57% (Smithies 1982). There was also a sharp rise in juvenile crime during the war that resulted in greater use of corporal punishment. Birching was meted out to 546 offenders in 1941 compared with just 58 in 1939 (Smith 1996: 17).

While some crimes decreased during the war (petrol rationing led to a sharp decline in the number of traffic offences – Calder 1971: 389), others increased sharply not least as a result of wartime regulations. As Gardiner (2004) explains, 'Some crimes were entirely specific to the situation of war: being unable to produce an identity card when required to, entering a restricted zone without a permit, rationing offences, "defeatist talk", absenteeism at work – and of course contravening blackout regulations' (p. 505). In addition, some crimes became 'more reprehensible' and attracted more severe sanctions as a result of wartime conditions. 'Reprehensible' wartime crimes included 'stealing food and goods from the workplace, sabotaging machinery involved in war production, taking advantage of the blackout to mug pedestrians, stealing from bombed-out properties' (p. 505).

There was also a rise in criminal activity amongst normally law-abiding citizens and public officials. The 'ugly phenomenon of looting' (Mackay 2002: 84) provides the most telling illustration of criminal activity of this kind. Following the first air raids in London, cases of looting increased from 539 in September 1940 to 1662 in the following month. As Thomas (2003) points out in *An Underworld at War*, much looting was of a relatively minor nature such as taking 'some tablets of soap from a bomb-damaged factory in Croydon'; absconding with 'two shoes from a damaged lock-up shop'; removing coal from a bombed out church in Holloway or making off with crockery 'from a bombed bungalow in Southend' (p. 81). Although most cases of looting were dealt with by local magistrates, who could impose prison terms of up to 12 months (the previous maximum of 3 months had been extended by an Order of 1940 – Smith 1996), this crime remained a capital offence under the Defence of the Realm Act. Cases remitted to the higher courts tended to attract more severe sentences, particular if they involved those who had abused a position of trust such as police

officers, ARP wardens, fire fighters or soldiers. In October 1940, an aux-
iliary fireman was 'sentenced to six months in prison for stealing three
lighters and a pipe from bomb-damaged premises' (Thomas 2003: 84),
while sixteen soldiers convicted of looting from homes in Kent in 1942 were
'handed down terms ranging from five years penal servitude to eight years
hard labour' (p. 80).

There were many other examples of anti-social crimes perpetrated by
public officials and professionals during the war. A Liverpool city councillor
was sent to prison for seven years and fined £2000 in 1942 for supplying
false documentation relating to the 'reserved' occupations of his business
employees (Gardiner 2004: 508). The Food Executive Officer in Barking
was sentenced to three years of penal servitude for issuing illegal permits for
sugar (Thomas 2003: 140–1). There were also a number of cases of medical
practitioners being struck off by the General Medical Council or prosecuted
for issuing false certificates that enabled patients to avoid conscription or
delay their return to active service (pp. 48–9).

Finally, professional criminals continued their activities much as before.
There was no let up in the number of robberies, racketeering and counter-
feiting, although the introduction of rationing did alter the 'pattern' of
crime with increased theft of items such as butter, bacon, sugar and cigar-
ettes. Professional criminals were also quick to exploit new opportunities
for illegal activity, such as pick-pocketing and pilfering at public shelters,
ransacking unguarded premises during the blackout and 'bomb larks'
(fraudulent claims for bomb damage – Thomas 2003).

Treatment of aliens and anti-Semitism

The wartime solidarity observed on the Home Front did not always extend
to 'aliens' or minorities. As Smith (1996) notes, 'If the war created a new
sense of social solidarity, it did not include Jews, blacks, the Irish, German
and Austrian refugees or Italians living in Britain' (p. 10).

In wartime conditions it would have been unrealistic to expect the public
to maintain positive attitudes towards those residing in Britain whose
allegiances appeared to be with the enemy. As Calder (1971) notes, 'the
most obvious targets for hatred' were the settled German community living
in Britain, as well as the 60,000 German and Austrian refugees who had fled
to Britain to escape Nazi persecution (p. 150). The initial 'liberal' phase of
internment, which came into effect in September 1939, seemed to meet with
general public approval. Around 600 German or Austrian nationals were
detained, while a further 9000 had restrictions placed on their movements.
Within a few months, however, public support for more stringent controls,
such as mass internment had intensified. This hardening of public opinion
can be linked to various factors. First, right-wing anti-alien press campaigns
were mounted by newspapers such as the *Daily Mail, Sunday Express,*

Sunday Dispatch and *Sunday Pictorial*. Secondly, the activities of refugee 'fifth columnists' were widely reported to have played a significant part in the successful German invasions of Norway and the Netherlands. In a BBC broadcast on 30 May 1940, Sir Nevile Bland, the government minister at The Hague, informed the British public that they should be suspicious of anyone with 'German and Austrian connections' (Kushner 1989: 146). Thirdly, official resistance to a policy of mass internment dissipated following concerted military pressure that a measure of this kind was needed to address the significant threat posed to national security by aliens. As a consequence, just over 27,000 aliens were interned by the end of June 1940 (see Lafitte 1944; Gillman and Gillman 1980).

The entry of Italy into the war in the same month led to mobs attacking the business premises of Italians in a number of British cities, such as London, Liverpool, Cardiff and Swansea. 'The worst violence took place in Glasgow, Clydebank and particularly in Edinburgh. *The Scotsman* reported smashing and looting in Leith Street with arson attacks, the crowd singing patriotic songs, people taken to hospital with head injuries, many arrests and rumours of a shopkeeper being killed' (Gardiner 2004: 223).

The war did little to foster more positive public attitudes towards the Jewish community in Britain. As Kushner (1989) points out, 'Strains of the phoney war, strains due to the threat of invasion, strains due to the hardships of rationing, strains of mass evacuation, strains of war weariness, all needed an outlet and the Jews were often a suitable scapegoat' (p. 194). Jewish people were liable to be accused of all forms of anti-social activity, including fleeing to the safest billets, evading the call-up, avoiding fire-watch duties, ostentatious displays of wealth and pushing to the front of queues (Calder 1971; McLaine 1979). Jewish wholesalers and retailers were also accused of controlling 'black markets'. Some Jewish traders, like their Gentile counterparts, were involved in illegality of this kind, but their 'un-British conduct attracted disproportionate publicity and greater opprobrium' (Kushner 1989). Unfounded rumours were even put about that 'panicking Jews' had caused the Bethnal Green tube station disaster in June 1943 in which 173 people lost their lives (Kushner 1989; Report on an Inquiry into the Accident at Bethnal Green Tube Station Shelter 1945).

Enemy propagandists and the British Union of Fascists whipped up anti-Semitic sentiments suggesting that Britain was fighting the war to defend the interests of Jewish capitalists. Lord Haw-Haw's broadcasts from Germany, which 'no fewer than 24 million' citizens admitted to listening to on an occasional basis (Hylton 2001: 181), often included derogatory references to Sir Izzy Myrgatroyd, a fictitious Jewish tax evader.

Official reticence to confront the issue of anti-Semitism during the war only served to increase its prevalence. Requests from the Jewish Board of Deputies for the government to take a more active stance in combating anti-Semitism were rebuffed on the grounds that pro-Jewish action of an 'official' kind would prove counter-productive (Kushner 1989).

Strikes and absenteeism

The idea that the experience of war would lead to greater industrial unity is hard to substantiate. The persistence of strike activity and absenteeism during the war years suggests that workers and employers were not pre-pared to set aside deep-rooted antagonisms in order to pursue national as opposed to class interests. Although the number of days lost through strike action decreased from 1939 to 1940, 'thanks to Dunkirk' (Calder 1971: 299), there was a steady increase in all the subsequent years of the war rising from 1,077,000 in 1941 to 3,696,000 by 1944 (Central Statistical Office 1995, Table 3.30, p. 64). Coal mining was by far the most strike prone industry 'accounting for two-thirds of the days lost in 1944' (p. 456). According to one Mass Observation report of the situation in factories in the north of England in 1941:

> one looked and listened in vain for any sign of a unity binding all parties in the fight against Germany. From the men, one got the fight against management. From the management one experienced hours of vituper-ation against the men. Both sides claim to be concerned only with improving the situation to increase the strength of the struggle against Fascism, but, nevertheless, the real war which is being fought here today is still pre-war, private and economic.
>
> (Quoted in Smith 1996: 45)

Although strikes had been made illegal under wartime regulations, there was a reluctance to enforce the law given the coalition government's desire to maintain good relations with the trade unions and avoid unnecessary confrontation. So, for example, when the Betteshanger colliery dispute was resolved in 1942, the Home Secretary moved quickly to ensure that the three imprisoned 'ringleaders' were released from custody and that no subsequent attempts were made to imprison strikers (Gardiner 2004: 516–17).

According to official estimates, absenteeism also increased in the period from 1941 to 1943 before levelling off in subsequent years (no figures were kept for the early years of the war). 'The average absence for men was 6 to 8% of man-hours worked and for women an average of 12 to 15%' (Mackay 2002: 121). The greater level of absenteeism amongst women reflected their additional responsibilities in relation to unpaid care and domestic tasks. As Mackay (2002) notes, the higher incidence of 'female absenteeism reveals less about commitment to victory than about the failure of employers and other family members to adjust their thinking to take account of the unequal burden that fell on so many women' (p. 123).

Younger people proved, however, to be the worst culprits in terms of absenteeism and time keeping. Some of the more persistent offenders were brought before the courts. A young factory worker, Dora Murrell, for example, was summoned to appear before Croydon Magistrates for 'being late for work on no fewer than 49 occasions and absent altogether on 2 days' (Waller 2005: 271). The defendant argued, unsuccessfully, that her poor time keeping had been due to her modest wages, which could not stretch to the purchase of a scarce and expensive item such as an alarm clock. 'A fine of £4 and £1 1s costs no doubt put the clock even further out of reach' (p. 271).

Unfair sacrifices

There was certainly a general feeling at the time that the contributions offered by or demanded from more affluent citizens in furtherance of the war effort were inadequate. There were suggestions that better-off families in the rural reception areas were able to use their influence to avoid being drawn into the evacuation scheme. Officials seemed reluctant to heed government advice about the need to operate the billeting scheme 'without fear or favour' if this ran the risk of antagonising influential local land-owners or dignitaries (McLaine 1979: 176). Furthermore, according to a Home Intelligence report of 1942, some members of the public held the view that rationing had less effect on the rich than 'ordinary' people. The rich it was argued were still able to eat at expensive restaurants (though they were, in theory, restricted to one main course from July 1940), purchase 'high priced goods in short demand, such as salmon and game', 'spend more on clothes and therefore use their coupons more advantageously', 'receive preferential treatment' from retailers because of their higher purchasing power and enjoy more plentiful supplies of petrol (quoted in Smith 1996: 47–8; see also Waller 2005). Some wealthy citizens even enjoyed enhanced protection during the air raids in London because many of the restaurants and clubs they frequented had deep underground basements. The Stepney Tenants Defence League organized a mass protest at the Savoy hotel during an air raid in September 1940 to highlight this particular inequity (Lewis 1986). Upper-class women also had the choice of being able to opt for voluntary, rather than paid work during the war. This enabled them not only to avoid being conscripted into the services or engaging in munitions work, but also allowed them to take time off whenever they liked (Smith 1996: 44).

Compiling the scorecard

Revisionist accounts of the impact of war on the Home Front provide a valuable counter-balance to some of the more rosy official accounts of civilian morale and behaviour during this era. Certainly, it is possible to challenge Titmuss' (1950) contention, outlined in his influential study *Problems of Social Policy*, that the experience of total war had led to a greater sense of social unity and to growing demands for government to play a leading role in creating a fairer post-war society.

One question that needs to be addressed is whether the evidence relating to anti-social behaviour and attitudes during the war is sufficiently strong to overturn the broad thrust of the Titmuss thesis. Might there be, as Lowe (2004a) reminds us, a danger that in focusing on the 'recorded failings of a few' we might overlook the unrecorded 'merits of the many'? (p. 619). Following an extensive review of the evidence, one contemporary scholar, Robert Mackay (2002), suggests that pro-social activity, such as volunteering 'far outweighed the negative features of civilian behaviour on the home front – absenteeism, strikes, looting, blackmarketeering and the like. The sheer bulk of volunteering should stand as a reminder to commentators that most people behaved well – many of them outstandingly well – in the trying conditions of war. The failings of the few are, of course, part of the history of the war, but they should never be allowed to obscure the merit of the many' (p. 133). This seems to be a reasonable conclusion to draw. The sacrifices made both by service personnel and those on the Home Front lend strong support to the notion that citizens were more willing to make greater efforts to help one another during the war.

Another question to resolve is whether this upsurge in community spirit led to deeper attitudinal changes amongst the British people. As was noted previously, there is evidence to suggest that there was a 'leftward' turn in the public's political outlook. Wartime experiences had alerted citizens to the ways in which government intervention could lead to more equitable economic and social conditions. Electing a reform orientated post-war government that was committed to improved living standards, full employment, social security, health care and enhanced educational opportunities for all, came to be seen as preferable to a return to rule by the 'guilty men' of yesteryear. Moreover, the war did seem to have increased the public's awareness of the commonality of human needs. State welfare provision was increasingly perceived not only as benefiting one's own family at a time of need, but also those of one's fellow citizens. This positive approach to state intervention was not confined to working class citizens. Growing numbers of middle-class citizens also believed that their life chances could be enhanced by a more interventionist government (McCullum and Readman 1964).

Of course, the increased level of public support for a fairer society was interpreted by some as indicative of a desire for a full bloodied version of democratic socialism. There was disappointment in post-war Labour circles when it became clear that the public's appetite for the creation of a peacetime socialist commonwealth based on the selflessness and co-operation that had emerged during wartime was limited.

The reconstruction of British society was one of the central issues for the wartime coalition government. The next section will revisit the question of whether the two main coalition parties shared a common vision of the role that social policy could play in this process of reconstruction.

Social policy and the coalition government 1940–45

According to one influential commentator, Paul Addison (1977), the Churchill coalition 'proved to be the greatest reforming administration since the Liberal government of 1905–14' (p. 14). The policies pursued by the coalition should not be regarded, he argues, as a pragmatic wartime accord. On the contrary, a 'massive new middle ground had arisen in politics. A species of consensus had existed between Stanley Baldwin and Ramsey MacDonald in the 1920s: a consensus to prevent anything unusual from happening. The new consensus of the war years was positive and purposeful' (p. 14). Others, however, take a contrary position. According to both Brooke (1992) and Smith (1996), although there were a number of important collaborative welfare initiatives during the war, these should *not* be regarded as evidence of a genuine convergence between the Conservatives and Labour during this time. The key question to consider here is whether the wartime reforms that were introduced by the coalition government can be viewed as uneasy compromises or the emergence of a more durable form of welfare consensus.

Although Labour recognized that the war would provide a unique opportunity to demonstrate the superiority of socialist ideas, such as state planning, they were unwilling to serve in Neville Chamberlain's initial wartime government preferring to remain as a constructive opposition party (Brooke 1992). However, when the tide turned against the Chamberlain administration, following the retreat of the British Expeditionary Force from Norway, Labour did agree to join Churchill's government in May 1940. Sixteen Labour members joined the government, of whom two, Attlee and Greenwood, were appointed to Churchill's war Cabinet.

Labour's decision to serve in Churchill's coalition government was based on a careful calculation that the benefits of this course of action would outweigh the costs. Participation would, for example, enable leading figures within the Party to gain invaluable administrative experience and to demonstrate to the public their suitability for office. By joining the coalition, Labour would also be in a much better position to influence the wartime political agenda, particularly in relation to social and economic reconstruction. On the downside, there was an undoubted risk that if Labour ministers were seen to be overly enthusiastic in their support for 'non-socialist' coalition policies on grounds of national unity they were liable to face severe criticism from rank and file members of their own party.

In practice, there were significant differences of opinion within the Party as to the underlying purpose of Labour's membership of the coalition.

While leading Labour members of the coalition, such as Attlee and Morrison wanted to push the government in a socialist direction, they acknowledged that there would be severe limits on how much they could achieve given Conservative domination of the administration. In contrast, those on the left of the parliamentary Party such as Laski, Bevan and Shinwell believed that the sole purpose of Labour's presence in government was to bring about significant socialist economic and social advance. Not surprisingly, perhaps, Labour ministers always tended to emphasize the progress they were making within the constraints of coalition government while their opponents in the wider Labour movement stressed their too ready acquiescence with Conservative policy objectives. In the economic sphere, for example, Labour ministers pointed to their success in nationalizing the fire service, and in establishing greater public control in relation to the railways and the coal industry. For many Labour backbenchers, half hearted reforms of this kind amounted to a betrayal of socialist principles. Full nationalization of both the railways and the coal industry were regarded as the minimum goals to be achieved if Labour's membership of the coalition was to be judged worthwhile (Brooke 1992). In terms of social policy, Labour's coalition ministers emphasized the positive role they had played in 'replacing' the household means test with an individual income test in 1941 and in securing an increase in old age pension allowances in 1942. For those on the left, though, these measures were deemed to be inadequate and indicative of a lack of true socialist resolve on the part of Labour ministers.

Up until the time of the publication of the Beveridge Report there had been limited progress in relation to the post-war economic and social reconstruction of society. Addison (1977) argues that this was due to the lack of drive on the part of Greenwood, the Labour minister with responsibility for reconstruction, to press ahead with the reform agenda. For Brooke (1992), in contrast, the lack of progress is better explained by the fact that the Reconstruction Priorities Committee lacked executive powers and by the pressing need to focus on the military campaign.

The Beveridge report

The reconstruction debate was ignited by the publication of the Beveridge Report in 1942. It proved to be a significant source of friction between Labour ministers and their own backbenchers. Although the latter believed that the Report was capable of improvement in several respects, they recognized that it had much in common with official Labour policy and were quick to offer their support. In particular, the backbenchers recognized the symbolic significance of the report and as such were keen to exploit this to the full. As Brooke (1992) notes, 'Some in the Labour Party went as far as to suggest that the struggle for the implementation of the Beveridge Report should be regarded as the struggle for socialism' (p. 147). While Labour ministers were enthusiastic about the Report, the Conservative members of the coalition were more circumspect. Churchill feared that implementing the Report's proposals would detract from the war effort (Jefferys 1994) and measures were taken to dampen down popular expectations. The publication of an Army Bureau of Current Affairs overview of the Report, for example, which included an introduction by Beveridge, caused consternation in official circles and was withdrawn from circulation by Sir James Gregg, the Secretary of War.

In response to Conservative anxieties, a compromise response to the Report was agreed, which left open the vague possibility of wartime implementation. Inevitably, this proved unsatisfactory to many Labour backbenchers. Despite concerted efforts by Morrison to head off a Labour 'rebellion', some 97 Labour backbenchers supported a motion condemning the government's stance on the Report at the end of a three-day debate in February 1943.

The Beveridge Report proved to be the catalyst for a more concerted emphasis on national reconstruction. By June 1943 Attlee, Bevin and Morrison had circulated a paper to Cabinet entitled 'The Need for Decisions', which set out the importance of implementing economic and social reform during wartime, rather than waiting until the nation's financial position had been assessed at the end of the war. As Brooke (1992) notes, 'The three urged decisions and the preparation of legislation on such questions as land and its use, building, water supply, reorganization of transport, heat and power, social security, education, agriculture, full employment, industry, export trade, health, and colonial policy' (p. 181). This pressure elicited a positive response from Conservative members of the coalition. In November 1943, a Ministry of Reconstruction was established under the direction of Lord Woolton. This proved to be highly significant in ensuring that reforms in social security, education and health moved up the political agenda.

While compromise agreements were reached in all these areas, it is important to recognize that the Conservatives tended to regard the proposed measures as the endpoint of a 'modernizing' process, while Labour viewed them as merely the first steps on the road to reform. Certainly, there are indications that many in the Labour movement had strong reservations about the direction of post-1943 coalition social policy. While the White Paper on social security published in September 1944 adhered to many of the prescriptions laid down by Beveridge, the coalition's unwillingness to agree to the introduction of subsistence benefit rates or open-ended benefit claims proved disappointing to many Labour supporters.

Education and health reforms

In the field of education, the 1944 Education Act was generally well received in Labour circles, although again it was seen as the first step in securing educational advance. The Act met Labour's two principal educational objectives. These were ensuring that all children had access to free secondary education tailored to their respective aptitudes and abilities and raising the school leaving age from 14 to 15 years. However, both the London Labour Party (LLP) and the National Association of Labour Teachers (NALT) expressed concerns that while 'The Act formally instituted a system of undifferentiated secondary education,' it 'informally enshrined a rigid tripartite structure' (Brooke 1992: 187). Assurances from Chuter Ede, the Labour Secretary of State at the Board of Education, that the Act would guarantee parity of status between grammar, modern and technical schools held little sway amongst either the LLP or NALT, who wanted to see the establishment of classless multilateral schools. Concerns were also raised about the failure to incorporate direct grant schools into the state scheme, as well as the unnecessary 'concessions made to denominational interests and the failure to set a date for the raising of the school-leaving age to 16' (p. 198).

There were even sharper divisions between Labour and the Conservatives over the question of health reform. The task of devising coalition health policy had fallen to the National Liberal MP Ernest Brown (until the Conservative Henry Willink replaced him in October 1943) and Tom Johnson the Labour Secretary of State for Scotland. The White Paper, *A National Health Service*, finally emerged in February 1944. Its original publication date had been delayed by Churchill at the last minute so that his two most loyal advisors, Brendan Bracken (the Minister of Information) and Max Beaverbrook (the Lord Privy Seal) could scrutinize the proposals to ensure that they did not undermine the Conservative standpoint (see Brooke 1992). The White Paper represented a decidedly uneasy compromise between the two Parties. For example, Labour's preference for the establishment of health centres staffed by salaried state doctors was tempered in the report by the recommendation that medical professionals working on a part-time basis in these centres would, like those who worked outside, continue to receive capitation fees. These payments were seen as preserving 'the sacrosanct link between doctor and patient with its notions of independence for the physician and free-choice for his or her client' (Hennessy 1993: 135). Predictably, the document failed to receive a ringing endorsement from either Labour or the Conservatives. Labour remained concerned about the continuation of capitation payments, the role of the voluntary hospitals and the prioritization of the interests of doctors over patients. Many Conservative supporters, not least those in the British Medical Association, objected to what they considered to be the first step towards a wholly salaried medical service and to the threat the White Paper posed to the autonomy of the voluntary hospitals. Indeed, such was the virulence of the Conservative/ professional response that Willink subsequently made a peace offering including an extension of the so-called panel system (under which insured patients could choose a doctor from a list of participating practitioners), as well as 'the establishment of a medical profession dominated bureaucracy, and, worst of all for Labour, the agreement that health centres were merely to be experimental' (Brooke 1992: 213; see also Jones 1999).

The coalition government: a phoney consensus?

Opinion remains divided over whether a welfare consensus emerged during the period of Churchill's coalition government. Both Addison and Lowe, for example, contend that this administration represented a staging post for the welfare consensus that lasted until the late 1970s. According to Addison (1977), the Attlee government of 1945 'had only to consolidate and extend the consensus achieved under the Coalition' (p. 261). Lowe (1990) argues that 'during the period of serious reconstruction planning between February 1943 and summer 1944, there was all-party consensus on both the ability of government to resolve the many problems which had bedevilled the interwar years and the broad principles by which reform in the medium term should be guided. The consensus covered all areas of welfare policy' (pp. 168–9).

While it can be argued that the Conservatives were prepared to accept increased state intervention during the war, they remained at best reluctant, pragmatic collectivists (see George and Wilding 1976). The wartime experience had convinced many Conservatives that increased interventionism was necessary to deal with the increase in the working class electorate and the changing 'structural needs of an advanced industrial economy' (Lowe 2005: 21). Such pragmatic adaptation should not, however, be seen as denoting a shift towards an ideological consensus with Labour over the need for profound economic and social change. Although ministers such as Butler were beginning to embrace a more interventionist form of Conservatism, there remained a deep seated opposition to collectivism *per se*. As Smith (1996) notes, 'The traditional view that the war stimulated a consensus on the expansion of state activity pays insufficient attention to the reaction against collectivism which intensified during the war's final years' (Smith 1996: 26). Several pressure groups emerged during the early 1940s with the expressed aim of defending the 'free enterprise' system. These included the Aims of Industry (1942), the Progress Trust and The Society for Individual Freedom (which was established in 1942 following the amalgamation of the National league of Freedom and the Society of Individualists). 'These groups were supported by prominent Conservatives, including Ralph Assheton, who became Conservative Party Chairman in 1944, A.G. Erskine-Hill, Chairman of the Conservative Party's back-bench 1922

Committee, and Henry Willink, the Minister of Health from 1943 to 1945' (p. 26).

While Labour members of the coalition government attempted to develop progressive, if not socialist, policies they were clearly frustrated by Churchill's limited enthusiasm for social reform, as well as the delaying tactics that he and other Conservative ministers employed to undermine the reconstruction agenda. The wartime 'accords' they entered into were not regarded either by Labour ministers or the Party more generally as evidence of a growing ideological consensus. As Brooke (1992) makes clear, 'a review of Labour's wartime approach to domestic reconstruction and the politics of coalition suggests that the consensus argument is a deeply flawed one' (p. 340).

Despite Labour's reservations about governing in coalition, the allied victory over Germany created a dilemma. Would the Party's longer-term interests be best served by a continuation of the coalition until victory over Japan had been assured or, at the very least, until a new electoral register had been compiled? While there was no question of Labour 'combining with the Conservatives on an electoral programme or participating in a "coupon" election' (Brooke 1992: 304), ministers such as Attlee and Bevin saw no urgent need for an early election believing that the continuation of the coalition might, in the event of a subsequent Conservative victory at the polls, prove to be the final opportunity to secure a further round of social reforms. It soon became apparent, however, that the magnitude of the gulf between the two parties over both economic and social policy was such that the coalition would inevitably come to an end. In May 1945, Churchill offered Labour the straight choice of continuing in coalition until the end of the Japanese conflict or an early General Election. Although Attlee, Dalton and Bevin were attracted to the former course of action, or some other compromise arrangements, strong opposition from the National Executive Committee led them to opt for a General Election. Following a brief 'caretaker' period of Conservative government (May–July 1945), a General Election was called for 5 July 1945.

The hard fought General Election campaign of 1945 shattered any illusion that party differences had narrowed during the war. There remained a huge gulf between the two parties over economic policy with the Conservatives favouring a speedy return to a free enterprise economy, while Labour stressed the need for public ownership, planning and controls. Although the Conservatives promised to introduce a National Insurance scheme, a comprehensive health service and a house building programme, these measures were presented as pragmatic reforms, rather than, as was the case with Labour, part of the transformation of society.

Conservative fears about Labour's alleged determination to install 'a permanent system of bureaucratic control, reeking of totalitarianism' (Dale 2000a: 68) were frequently raised during the election campaign. Indeed, the Conservative chairman, Ralph Assheton, was so convinced of the need to alert the electorate to the imminent danger of Labour's totalitarian inclinations that he decided to donate one and a half tons of the Party's 'precious paper assignment for the general election campaign' to the publisher Routledge so that additional abridged copies of Hayek's influential anti-collectivist text, *The Road to Serfdom*, could be published before the election (Cockett 1995: 93). In his infamous first election broadcast on 4 June 1945, Churchill asserted that the election of a socialist government would lead to 'an attack on the right to breathe freely without having a harsh, clumsy, tyrannical hand clasped across the mouth and nostrils'. Labour, he declared, would have to 'fall back on some form of Gestapo' in order to curb 'free, sharp, or violently worded expressions of public discontent' (quoted in Kramnick and Sheerman 1993: 481).

Throughout the campaign, both Churchill and Beaverbrook sought to persuade the electorate not to be 'hoodwinked' by the apparent reasonableness of Labour's leadership, arguing that it was the 'alien' and unaccountable influence of the Party's chairman, Harold Laski, which would dictate the policy agenda of a post-war Labour government.

Labour vigorously rejected such assertions arguing that it was only a democratic socialist government that could bolster personal freedom, and provide an effective challenge to the monopoly power and profiteering that were endemic features of an unregulated capitalism. They also reminded the electorate that they were the only party who were enthusiastic supporters of the welfare state and economic interventionism. In the event, it was Labour's message that resonated with the public (see Adelman 1986). As Kramnick and Sheerman (1993) conclude:

> the Tories were seen as the party of Munich, and Labour, not as wild revolutionaries but as efficient managers who had proved they could 'get the job done' in their wartime ministries. The forced sharing and mutual suffering of the war had produced a communal climate responsive to Labour's electoral message of a better-planned egalitarian society with full employment and improved social benefits for all.
>
> (p. 490)

In summary, it is hard to dispute the claim that the Second World War had a positive impact on social attitudes thereby generating support for more egalitarian forms of state intervention. The suggestion that the wartime coalition government operated on the basis of a consensus is much harder to substantiate. Although Labour and Conservative members of the wartime coalition government reached 'agreement' over a number of social policy initiatives this did not, as the General Election campaign of 1945 demonstrated, amount to an ideological consensus.

In the next chapter, the democratic socialist approach to social policy adopted by the Labour governments from 1945 to 1951 will be revisited.

Further reading

There are a number of useful sources which examine the social impact of the Second World War on the civilian population. These include Titmuss' (1950) official wartime history, arguably his finest work, as well as influential accounts by Harrison (1978), Calder (1971, 1992) and Harold Smith (ed.) (1986, 1996). Mackay (2002) has written a highly readable and informative account of morale on the Home Front. Addison (1977), Brooke (1992) and Jefferys (1994) provide contrasting assessments of Churchill's wartime coalition government.

chapter

two

Revisiting the Labour Governments 1945–1951: towards a Democratic Socialist Welfare State and society?

Despite the fact that the polling organization Gallup predicted a Labour victory in the run up to the General Election of 1945, there was still a sense of disbelief in many quarters when it was finally confirmed that it would be Attlee, rather than Churchill, who would be leading Britain's first post-war government (Hennessy 1993: chapter 2). From a modest showing in the 1935 General Election (in which Labour secured just 154 out of a possible 617 seats with 38% of the votes), the Party swept to power in 1945 winning 393 seats (out of 604) increasing its share of the vote to 48% (Harmer 1999). Labour now had the opportunity to carry through its pledge to create the democratic socialist society that it had outlined in its General Election manifesto, *Let Us Face the Future*:

> The Labour Party is a Socialist Party, and proud of it. Its ultimate purpose at home is the establishment of the Socialist Commonwealth of Great Britain – free, democratic, efficient, progressive, public-spirited, its material resources organized in the service of the British people.
>
> (Labour Party 1945: 6)

For Labour, democratic socialism amounted to something more than the humane modification of capitalist society. The party wanted to create an egalitarian and solidaristic society by gradual, constitutional means. The first phase of this transformation would involve the nationalization of key industries, state regulation of the economy, progressive taxation and the introduction of an egalitarian welfare state.

The first part of this chapter will be devoted to an examination and assessment of Labour's democratic socialist welfare programme during their first term in office (1945–50). Attention will then be given to Labour's economic policies during this period, which formed an equally important part of its socialist strategy. The chapter will conclude with a review of Labour's embrace of consolidation during its second term in office (1950–51).

Creating a Democratic Socialist Welfare State

Questions have been raised as to whether Attlee's democratic socialist government 'established' the welfare state. In Pearce's (1994) estimation 'Labour's achievement was more one of modernizing, improving and greatly extending an existing structure than of building an entirely new edifice' (p. 46). Certainly, there were some notable state welfare initiatives in the earlier part of the twentieth century, not least during the period of Liberal rule between 1906 and 1914 (Gilbert 1970; Hay 1983). Subsequently, as Digby (1989) reminds us, there were even 'significant advances in inter-war social policy' – an era often characterized as a 'welfare wasteland' (p. 48). Crucially, however, these developments were not based on any clear ideology or over-arching goals. Searle's (2001) description of the Liberal reforms as a 'patchwork quilt of *ad hoc* measures based on no single principle or philosophy, and sometimes colliding with one another' (p. 94) could readily be applied to these early welfare initiatives.

Some commentators such as Addison (1997) have suggested that the modern welfare state was created by Churchill's wartime coalition government.

> Social security for all, family allowances, major reform in education, a National Health Service, Keynesian budgetary technique, full employment policies, town and country planning, closer relations between the state and industry – all these had been set on foot by the spring of 1943. By the spring of 1945 a new and wide-ranging prospectus of peacetime development was at an advanced stage of preparation within the civil service, while educational reform had already been embodied in the Butler Act of 1944 and only had to be administered. All three parties went to the polls in 1945 committed to principles of social and economic reconstruction which their leaders had endorsed as members of the Coalition. A massive new middle ground had arisen in politics.
>
> (p. 14)

Others have contested this view, believing that Labour's post-1945 welfare reforms were underpinned by distinctive democratic socialist principles (Brooke 1992; Francis 1997; Smith 2000). As Jefferys (1992) points out, 'Wartime developments had helped to create a new intellectual climate, one more favourable to state welfare than had existed in the 1930s, but the shape and extent of reform still owed much to Labour's tradition of democratic socialism' (p. 23).

Social Security

The Labour Party had a long-standing commitment to the abolition of poverty and social security for all. At the Party conference of 1942 'a comprehensive scheme of social security' was endorsed prior to the publication of the Beveridge Report (Pearce 1994: 48). James Griffiths, the new Minister of National Insurance in the Attlee government, acted speedily to secure the necessary funds (£59 million) from Dalton in order to implement the Family Allowances Act (which had been introduced by Churchill's caretaker government in May 1945). He then piloted the Industrial Injuries Act through the Commons in 1946, under which the state, rather than employers and private insurers, assumed responsibility for compensating those injured at work.

The National Insurance Act of 1946 was the cornerstone of Labour's social security programme. Under this tripartite funded scheme, everyone 'from the barrow boy to the field marshal' (Griffiths 1969: 84) who made the requisite flat-rate contributions was entitled to claim a range of flat-rate benefits (unemployment benefit, sickness benefit, dependants' allowances, maternity payments, retirement pensions and a death grant) at time of need.

The final element in Labour's programme of social security was the National Assistance Act of 1948, which provided means-tested payments for those who did not qualify for National Insurance benefits. These safety net benefits were to be administered by a newly established National Assistance Board rather than local authority Public Assistance Committees.

Labour's social security reforms represented a significant improvement on pre-war arrangements. The reforms drew heavily from the recommendations contained in the Beveridge Report on Social Insurance, although there were some notable differences. Beveridge's call to phase in the new retirement pensions over a 20-year period on cost-saving grounds was rejected because of the need to deal swiftly with the financial needs of existing pensioners. As Timmins (2001) notes, full pensions were introduced 'within three months of the 1946 Act becoming law and although it was a mighty expensive decision, almost certainly nothing else would have been politically tenable' (p. 136). Labour was less enamoured though with Beveridge's proposals for 'an inexhaustible unemployment scheme, with provisions for compulsory training to apply to the long-term unemployed' (Hill 1993: 29). The Chancellor, Hugh Dalton, believed that this would prove too costly and persuaded the Cabinet to limit payment to a period of 180 days. Beveridge's innovative proposals for insured housewives (furniture grant upon marriage, domestic assistance during illness and an 'end of marriage' allowance) were also rejected on grounds of both cost and practicality.

Labour's decision to persevere with a National Insurance scheme (based on regressive flat rate contributions) meant that only those in paid work could exercise the right to claim benefits from this source. Although support, in the form of National Assistance, was provided for the non-insured, Labour did not depart from Beveridge's dictum that assistance 'must be felt to be something less desirable than insurance benefit; otherwise the insured persons get nothing for their contributions. Assistance therefore will be given always subject to proof of needs and examination of means' (Cmd 6404 1942, para. 369: 141). While these reforms could technically be said to have brought about an end to the Poor Law, the fact that some citizens would still be required to undergo a means-test to establish their eligibility for lower-level allowances represents a failure to recognize the subtleties of the problem of stigma (Page 1984).

Although the National Insurance benefit rates that Labour introduced were higher than those proposed in the coalition government's White Paper of 1944 (Cmd 6527 1944), they were relatively less generous than those advocated by Beveridge. This made it difficult to provide claimants with a guarantee of a 'subsistence' living standard. Although committed to limiting the role of means-testing in the new social security scheme, this proved difficult to realize in practice. The 'subsistence' National Insurance rates proved inadequate for those claimants with high housing costs. By 1948 some 675,000 recipients of National Insurance were claiming additional means-tested National Assistance benefits (which included a full rent allowance) in order to maintain a basic living standard.

In providing citizens with protection against the 'most abject destitution of the 1930s' (Jefferys 1992: 21), Labour's social security reforms can be regarded as a significant step forward. They could not, however, be regarded as the epitome of a democratic socialist form of social security. A number of modifications in both the design and operation of the system would be needed to achieve this objective such as making the eligibility criteria more generous, raising benefit levels and reviewing the income needs of those outside the labour market.

The National Health Service

The National Health Service has come to be regarded as the most notable achievement of the Attlee governments (Webster 2002). Prior to 1948 medical care had been restricted to the better off and those covered by the National Insurance scheme of 1911 or by virtue of trade union or friendly society membership. Under the pre-war National Insurance arrangements, around 20 million workers (although not their dependants) were provided with basic financial protection, the services of a General Practitioner (GP) selected from a designated list (the panel system) and limited specialist provision. As Brooke (1992) notes, 'Such deficiencies were compounded by the lack of a unified hospital system; the privately run voluntary and publicly run municipal institutions operated side by side, with no semblance of co-ordination' (p. 134).

Spurred on by the Socialist Medical Association, Labour sought to provide a tax funded, democratically accountable, universal health care service free at the point of delivery on a citizenship basis. A system of health centres staffed by groups of full-time salaried medical practitioners was to be established and hospital provision was to be unified. Capitation fees for GPs were rejected because they were based on competition rather than co-operation and the sale of medical practices was to be phased out (Brooke 1992; Stewart 1999).

Although there was cross-party agreement about the need for reform, significant differences remained about the best way to proceed. The coalition government's White Paper of 1944 *A National Health Service* (Cmd 6502 1944) attempted, but ultimately failed, to reconcile some of the differences in relation to payments, professional autonomy and organizational control.

Labour's new Minister of Health, Aneurin Bevan, was determined to establish a National Health Service in which high standard comprehensive provision was to be made freely available to all citizens. His decision to nationalize the hospitals represented a major departure from the coalition government's health strategy. In order to achieve this objective, Bevan recognized that he would have to secure the co-operation of hospital consultants. He achieved this by offering them generous salaries thereby freeing 'them from the necessity to drum up business from GPs and rich clients to pay for their basic income' (Glennerster 2007: 51). Additional merit awards were proposed 'to compensate for any loss of private earnings and reward excellence in their professional accomplishments' (Webster 2002: 26) and the right of consultants to engage in private work (pay beds were to be permitted in NHS hospitals) was accepted. In addition, the consultants were to be granted significant representation within the new NHS administrative structures while the distinctive position of teaching hospitals was to be preserved by means of separate governing arrangements.

General medical practitioners, who were highly influential within the British Medical Association, were less enamoured by Bevan's reforms. They objected to the possibility, however remote, that they might eventually become salaried state employees, rather than independent contractors and to the prohibition on the sale of medical practices. They were also uneasy about the 'oppressive' administrative arrangements of the new service that would permit medical personnel to be 'directed' to 'under-doctored' localities. Although the legislation came onto the statute book in 1946, it was not until a few weeks before the service was due to become operational on the 'appointed day' (5 July 1948) that the GPs, after protracted negotiations, agreed to join the new service. Bevan's decision to accept amending legislation that effectively ruled out the possibility of introducing a salaried profession through the 'back door' proved to be decisive in this regard.

The concessions that Bevan made on a salaried service, medical centres and pay beds have been seen by some as a high price to pay for the establishment of a National Health Service (see Campbell 1994: chapter 12; Stewart 1999). There are good grounds, however, for contending that these compromises were a necessary price to pay for securing a significant improvement in health care provision, not least for the poorer members of society. As Francis (1997) concludes, the

> new medical service which Bevan had helped to establish had been moulded in accordance with a number of priorities which he understood to be distinctly socialist. The NHS fulfilled the principles of universalism, comprehensiveness, and funding from central taxation. It had also sought to establish that health care should be seen as an inalienable right, rather than a commodity whose provision was dependent on the vagaries of the market.
>
> (pp. 113–14)

Housing

In the Party's 1945 manifesto, housing was identified as 'one of the greatest and one of the earliest tests of a Government's real determination to put the nation first. Labour's pledge is firm and direct – it will proceed with a housing programme with the maximum practical speed until every family in this island has a good standard of accommodation' (Labour Party 1945: 8). This proved to be a demanding goal for a number of reasons. First, the post-war housing stock was in a poor condition. It was estimated that some 200,000 houses had been destroyed during the war while a further 250,000 had been made uninhabitable. Moreover, many of the habitable homes required urgent repairs of various kinds (Jones and Lowe 2002: 157–8). Secondly, there was an upsurge in the demand for housing as millions of servicemen and servicewomen returned home, many of whom were keen to form families. Thirdly, there was a shortage of both building materials (much of which had to be imported) and skilled construction workers.

Bevan (whose ministerial responsibilities encompassed housing, as well as health) believed that centrally subsidized, local authority house building for rent represented the best way to meet the growing demand for housing in post-war Britain. Although Bevan recognized the importance of building as many new homes as possible, he was not prepared to sacrifice quality for quantity. As Francis (1997) notes, Bevan 'insisted that new council homes should be buildings of a much higher standard than had previously been postulated for municipal housing. He was unapologetic in his belief that the working class had as much right to live in quality housing as the middle class' (p. 127). For Bevan the construction of spacious, albeit more costly, council houses that would stand the test of time was infinitely preferable to building more homes of a lower standard. Bevan justified his preference for a Treasury subsidized, local authority-led housing drive on the grounds that it would best meet the needs of those on low incomes who could not afford to take out a mortgage or pay high private sector rents. The greater availability of rented accommodation would also promote labour mobility given that owner occupiers were often unable to move to a new job because of difficulties in selling their existing property (see Francis 1997).

Bevan has been criticized for his ideological opposition to the construction of private homes for sale (Campbell 1994; see also Francis 1997), neglect of the privately rented sector (Glennerster 2007: 67), administrative failures, 'over-reliance on privately owned building firms to deliver production' (Malpass 2003: 600) and insufficient house completions (only 1 million houses had been built by 1951, instead of a projected 4 or 5 million). However, as Campbell (1994) notes, 'There was in truth no way that any Minister, in the economic conditions prevailing after 1945, could have met in full either the real housing need which the war had left behind or the inflated expectations which Labour had aroused during the General Election' (p. 153).

One other feature of Labour's housing policy should also be noted as it also reflected the Party's desire to create better living conditions for the British public. Although not mentioned in the Party's 1945 manifesto, an ambitious New Town programme, which was to become 'one of the great successes of post-war planning' (Timmins 2001: 147) was introduced in 1946. Fourteen new towns development corporations (including one chaired by Beveridge in Peterlee) were to be established from Crawley in Sussex to East Kilbride in Scotland (Hennessy 1993).

Finally, while it is difficult to take issue with Morgan's (1984) overall assessment that Labour's housing policy was 'competent', rather than 'outstanding' (p. 169), it is important not to overlook Bevan's achievements in this sphere. As Jefferys (1992) makes clear, 'Bevan's house-building programme meant that affordable, decent accommodation was, as never before, within the reach of thousands of lower-income families' (p. 61).

Education

Labour members of Churchill's coalition, most notably Chuter-Ede, had played a significant role in securing the passage of the 1944 Education Act (Bailey 1995). This reform was not regarded by the post-war Labour government as an uneasy compromise that would subsequently need to be imbued with a more distinctive democratic socialist character. Both of Attlee's education ministers, Ellen Wilkinson (1945–47) and George Tomlinson (1947–51) believed that adherence to the principle of 'equality of educational opportunity' and the introduction of 'free secondary education for all' (Francis 1997: 149) were the key elements of a democratic socialist education policy. They were not opposed, for example, to the competitive academic selection procedures favoured by the grammar schools provided that working class children had the same chance of success as their middle- and upper-class counterparts. Similarly, they supported the tripartite schooling system (grammar, technical and modern) provided that pupils were allocated to such schools on the basis of their skills and aptitude, rather than their social background. Although pupils would receive different types of education, there were to be no differences of esteem between the three kinds of school. In the more integrated society that Labour was seeking to create, it was envisaged that the technician and the craftsman would eventually enjoy equal status with the doctor or lawyer (Francis 1997).

Wilkinson and Tomlinson believed that their principal task as Education ministers was to ensure that 'the Butler Act of 1944, with its tripartite division of secondary schools' was implemented successfully (Morgan 1992: 40–41) and that the school leaving age was extended. This proved an uphill task. Wilkinson, for example, had to battle with Cabinet colleagues such as Cripps and Morrison in order to obtain the resources for the additional teachers and new buildings required to extend the school leaving age to 15 by 1947 (see Morgan 1984: 75–6).

Overall, it was, as Morgan (1984) notes, 'hard to avoid the view that education was an area where the Labour government failed to provide any new ideas or inspiration' (p. 177). While Labour's efforts to ensure that all children, regardless of means, should be able to continue in full-time education until the age of 15 was a step forward, their failure to grasp the deep rooted impact of class factors in determining the type of school that pupils attended or the socially divisive impact of a tripartite system of schooling represented significant oversights.

There were two spheres in education in which one might have expected Labour to pursue a more overtly democratic socialist approach. First, they could have given more support to the establishment of multilateral or comprehensive schools, not least in the light of growing criticisms about middle class capture of the grammar schools and the deficiencies in secondary modern education, where pupils were denied the opportunity of sitting external examinations. Although both Wilkinson and Tomlinson 'were willing to allow comprehensive *schools* to be set up as an experiment, they certainly had no desire to see the establishment of a national comprehensive *system*' (Francis 1997: 144–5). The main advocate of comprehensive education was the National Association of Labour Teachers (NALT). NALT believed that the best way to achieve greater social cohesion was through common schooling, which they contended was official Party policy citing conference resolutions passed in 1942 and 1946. It was not, however, until 1950 that an unambiguous resolution committing the Party to comprehensivization was finally passed at conference (see Francis 1997). A subsequent pamphlet, *A*

Policy for Secondary Education (Labour Party 1951b), set out the short-comings of the tripartite system, but it was only after Labour left office in 1951 that the case for comprehensive schooling was embraced within the Party.

Second, Labour had proved reluctant to tackle the thorny issue of private schooling, which had 'long been the entry gate to the class elite that ran British society' (Glennerster 2007: 140). The fact that a number of influential cabinet ministers were enthusiastic former pupils of these elitist institutions provides one explanation for the government's reluctance to initiate reform in this area. Indeed, Beckett (2000) contends that Attlee's devotion to his former school was such that he saw nothing wrong with offering ministerial preferment to Old Haileyburians, 'other things being equal' (p. 211). It was also believed that any direct attempt to abolish private schools would prove counter productive given limited public appetite for such reform. Rapid improvement in the quality of state education was seen as the best way to challenge the pre-eminence of the private schools. Once better-off parents came to recognize that there was no longer any advantage to be gained by educating their children privately the demand for fee-paying schools would rapidly decline.

Labour's success in establishing the post-war welfare state was a remarkable achievement. It should be remembered that their plans for the welfare state were constrained by the perilous state of the post-war economy. Britain had incurred wartime debts of £3000 million and was heavily dependent on US financial support in the form of Lend-Lease, which ended abruptly following the Japanese surrender in 1945 (see Morgan 1984). Exports stood at just one-third of their pre-war level and 40% of overseas markets had been lost. While Labour was forced to introduce a more 'austere' welfare programme than they would have wished, this still represented a significant advance in terms of both security and opportunity for British citizens (Tomlinson 1998).

Labour's Democratic Socialist economic strategy

Labour's economic strategy was 'designed' to end the inefficiency of unregulated free market activity and to ensure that production and distribution operated in ways that were compatible with the egalitarian vision of democratic socialism. Public ownership and planning were seen as two key ways to achieve these objectives.

Public ownership

Nationalization had been an integral part of Labour's socialist economic strategy since 1918 (Thompson 1996). Not surprisingly, therefore, the Party's manifesto of 1945 contained specific pledges to take the fuel and power industries, inland transport, as well as iron and steel into public ownership. These measures were seen as contributing to economic efficiency in a number of ways. According to Part IV of the Party's General Election manifesto the nationalization of gas and electricity, for example, would result in 'lower charges, prevent competitive waste, open the way for co-ordinated research and development, and lead to the reforming of uneconomic areas of distribution' (Labour Party 1945: 6). Nationalization of the transport system was also deemed necessary to prevent a private monopoly operating in ways which would be 'a menace to the rest of industry' (p. 7).

Nationalization was also seen as an important way of creating a more equal society. As Francis (1997) notes, unlike the Conservatives who 'were unwilling to see nationalization applied to more than one or two ailing industries, Labour saw public ownership of key industries and services as an inherently superior form of economic organization, which would allow working men and women to exercise full control of their own destinies' (p. 65). The control exercised by a small class of anti-social, self-interested capitalists over key sectors of the economy would give way to co-operative, democratic institutions that served the interest of the nation as a whole. In this way economic power would be redistributed 'both within industry and within society as a whole' (p. 74).

After coming to power in 1945 Labour moved swiftly to implement its nationalization proposals. By 1949 a fifth of the British economy was under direct public control. The Bank of England, Cable and Wireless, coal and civil aviation were nationalized in 1946. Electricity and inland transport followed in 1947 and gas in 1948. Finally, and more controversially, the iron and steel industries were nationalized in 1949.

In practice, nationalization tended to be promoted on grounds of economic efficiency rather than of equality. The fact that the Party opted for what came to be known as the Morrisonian model of public ownership (see Dell 1999: 143–5) accentuated this trend. Under this model, newly nationalized industries were granted considerable autonomy. They were expected to operate efficiently and to deliver profits. Although there was an expectation that workers within these industries would be more closely consulted about operational matters, the idea that workers should be guaranteed places on public boards or be able to exercise meaningful forms of control withered away. As Coates (1975) explains:

> The Nationalization Acts explicitly stated that 'expert' managers would be appointed by the responsible Minister, that these managers would be answerable not to the labour force within the industry but to the Minister and hence to Parliament, and that they would be expected to manage their nationalized industry in the spirit of business efficiency. These managerial cadres were to negotiate with trade unions . . . but the

trade unions, and the work forces that they represented, were not to become involved in traditional managerial prerogatives.

(p. 48)

The nationalization of the iron and steel industries highlighted the issue of whether this form of ownership should be based purely on the issue of efficiency or socialist principle. The decision to include the nationalization' of iron and steel in the Party manifesto of 1945 had been controversial. Without a 'rank-and-file rebellion' at the Party's annual conference in 1944 it is unlikely that this pledge would have been included in the manifesto (Brooke 1995: 19). Further controversy arose over the implementation of this commitment, with Morrison contending that the efficiency case for nationalization was unproven while the Iron and Steel Workers Union saw no need for a measure of this kind. In contrast, others argued that the failure to press ahead with the nationalization of these industries would give rise to serious doubts about 'the party's commitment to socialism' (p. 20).

This issue aroused heated debate in Cabinet and Attlee had to use his considerable skills to ensure that the measure was adopted (Pearce 1997: 147–8). Legislation was introduced in 1949, although it was 'agreed' to postpone the 'vesting' day until after the General Election of 1950 (see Morgan 1984; Thorpe 2001).

Importantly, the iron and steel debate served to highlight the growing internal divisions within the Labour Party between the more pragmatically minded 'consolidators', who believed that any additional measures of public ownership should be put on hold while a proper evaluation of the impact of the first round of such measures was undertaken and the more idealistic 'deep' socialists who believed that further rounds of nationalization were an essential feature of Labour's transformative doctrine (Jones 1996). The main problem for those attempting to defend public ownership on grounds of socialist principle was that the public corporation model put in place:

> . . . did not spark much interest, excitement, or loyalty. Even within the long-beleaguered coal industry, the jubilation at nationalization seems to have faded quite quickly. To some critics and workers, no difference between public ownership under Labour and private ownership under the Conservatives could be perceived. It had certainly not transformed the nature of the workplace.
>
> (Brooke 1995: 20)

Economic planning

Planning was the other key complementary element in Labour's democratic socialist economic strategy. As with public ownership there were differences of opinion within the Party over the precise goals of economic planning, as well as the policy instruments that should be used.

There were some within the Party, such as G.D.H. Cole (1950), Bevan and Laski, who held the view that the objective of democratic socialist planning was to ensure that there was an adequate supply of essential resources and that these should be distributed on the basis of need, rather than through the operation of the market. Those adhering to this doctrine were inclined to press for 'the continuation of the extensive physical controls inherited from wartime: controls over manpower, location of industry, the exchange mechanism, and supplies of raw materials and foodstuffs' (Francis 1997: 31). In contrast, there were those such as Jay (1937) and Durbin (1940), who believed that socialist objectives could be achieved without recourse to the directive microeconomic approach of the 'physical' planners. Influenced by Keynesian ideas, these members of the Labour Party believed it would be possible to use monetary and fiscal means to ensure that the market operated along 'socialist' lines. The main aim of this macro-economic approach to planning was to secure a non-inflationary form of full employment (Thompson 1996). Significantly, this latter perspective permitted a greater role for the price mechanism. Although some have questioned the socialist propensities of macroeconomic planning (Coates 1975; Howell 1976), it seems clear that in areas such as food subsidies and taxation Labour was attempting to steer policy in an egalitarian direction (see Morgan 1984; Whiting 2000).

It has been suggested that from around 1947 Labour began to rely more on budgetary rather than physical planning (Cairncross 1985). This was not, however, a 'straightforward shift'. The 'increasing resort to budgetary planning was paralleled by a continued insistence on the necessity of retaining strategic physical controls' (Francis 1997: 37).

A Democratic Socialist economic strategy?

Although some commentators such as Barnett (1986) and Dell (1999) have been highly critical of the Attlee government's failure to confront what they considered to be the underlying deficiencies of the British economy, such as low productivity, restrictive trade union practices and under investment, others take a more positive view (Morgan 1984; Jefferys 1992; Tomlinson 1997a). Despite the abrupt ending of Lend-Lease, the fuel and convertibility crises of 1947, Labour managed, with the assistance of American and Canadian loans (which were finally repaid at the end of 2006), to revitalize a war damaged economy through interventionist means. Inflation was kept under control, industrial production increased by a third between 1946 and 1951, exports outstripped imports, productivity rose and a growth rate of 3% per annum was achieved. The maintenance of full employment, except during the difficult winter of 1946–47, was a major achievement. 'In 1948, for instance, no more than 359,000 persons were unemployed in any single month (with only 299,000 in the best month), compared with 1,912,000 unemployed in the worst month of 1938, and nearly three million unemployed in 1932' (Rubinstein 2003: 239).

Labour's economic policy during this period was certainly underpinned by a democratic socialist ethos. However, they remained uncertain about how to transform the economy along socialist lines in the longer term. Was the Party's constitutional commitment to the abolition of capitalism still a long-term objective or could it be reformed to serve the public interest? With 50% of the nation's wealth still in the hands of just 1% of the population after five years of a Labour government, what further action should be taken to combat such gross inequalities?

By the end of its first term in office, Labour had made significant progress in moving both economic and social policy in a democratic socialist direction. Its resolution in pursuing its welfare agenda, given the extreme economic pressures it faced, is particularly noteworthy. While the Party's achievements may have been overstated in its General Election manifesto of 1950, it is hard to deny that real progress had been achieved:

> Labour has honoured the pledge it made in 1945 to make social security the birthright of every citizen. Today destitution has been banished. The best medical care is available to everyone in the land. Great Acts of Parliament – the National Insurance, Industrial Injuries, National Assistance and National Health Service Acts – have been placed on the Statute Book. This social legislation has benefited *all* sections of the community, including members of the middle classes. Hundreds of thousands of middle class and professional families have been relieved of one of their worst anxieties – the fear of the sudden illness, the expensive operation, the doctor's crippling bills.
>
> (Labour Party 1950: 8)

Labour's democratic socialist project seemed, however, to stall in the late 1940s. According to Pearce (1994), Labour's focus had been on 'remedying the evils of the past', rather than constructing a 'challenging agenda for the future' (p. 77).

The social conservatism of the Party leadership provides one explanation as to why Labour's 'crusade' ran out of steam by the end of the 1940s. The Attlee government displayed little appetite, for instance, for 'constitutional' reform. According to Morgan (1984), 'It showed a conservative attitude towards the civil service, and almost a reverence for the constitution, from the monarchy and the House of Lords to the fabric of local government which remained much as Lord Salisbury had left it in 1888' (pp. 493–4). Indeed, Labour made only two constitutional changes of note during its first term of office. In 1948 it introduced the Representation of the People Act, which abolished both university seats in parliament and the additional voting rights accorded to 'those who owned businesses outside their constituency of residence' (Pearce 1994: 76).

Legislation restricting the delaying powers of the House of Lords was introduced a year later.

Attlee's attachment to tradition expressed itself in a number of ways. His devotion to the monarchy was such that he allowed himself to be influenced by George VI's 'preferences' with regard to the appointment of the Foreign Secretary in 1945 (Pimlott 1985: chapter xxiv), as well as the timing of the 1951 General Election (Beckett 2000). Attlee's 'establishment' values also came to the fore in other ways, such as advising Bevan about the importance of wearing a dinner jacket, rather than a lounge suit to 'a smart event' (Beckett and Beckett 2004).

The conservatism of the Attlee government was also evident in terms of how it responded to other social issues. Given the primacy attached to class as a source of personal identity and the 'masculine' ethos within the Party, it is not surprising that Labour made little headway in responding to the specific needs of women (Francis 2000). In part, this was due to a belief that gender inequalities would fade away with the creation of the new socialist society. As Francis (1997) notes, 'for men (and indeed most women) in the Labour Party at this time "women's issues" were a distraction from the struggle to build socialism' (p. 212). Labour's pursuit of full employment and state welfare provision was intended to benefit both men and women. While Labour was minded to recognize the 'extreme toil and drudgery which characterized the lives of working-class housewives' (p. 209) by means of 'better housing, welfare and full employment for their husbands' (p. 210), there was much less sympathy for the complaints raised by what were seen as self-interested, leisured middle-class women in relation to food queues or 'the problem of finding, or keeping, domestic servants' (Francis 2000: 203).

The Labour government's limited interest in women's issues was particularly marked in the case of equal pay. While equal pay was accepted in principle, implementation was deemed problematic on the grounds of the inflationary consequences of boosting women's wages, the threat to free collective bargaining, and the need to 'compensate' men for their more onerous financial obligations towards other family members. Labour's lukewarm approach in this sphere was exploited by the Conservatives, who promised in their 1950 election manifesto to introduce equal pay for equal work for all government employees when the 'country's financial position' had improved as they envisaged (Dale 2000a: 80). It seems likely that female-orientated policies of this kind contributed to subsequent Conservative success in capturing women's votes in the 1950s and beyond (Zweiniger-Bargielowska 1996; Black and Brooke 1997).

The Attlee government's approach to racial inequalities also lacked a radical edge, in part, one suspects, because of the hostility of some members of the parliamentary party and the trade union movement towards immigrants from the New Commonwealth (see Thorpe 2001: 119). Moreover,

No action was taken over apartheid in South Africa or to improve the civic and social status of coloured immigrants from the Commonwealth at home. The Cabinet did discuss, on 20 March 1950, the problems encountered by West Indian immigrants over jobs, housing, and racial discrimination, but no legislative action was proposed.

(Morgan 1984: 56; see also Lunn 1993)

Labour's reluctance to ensure that key social institutions were imbued with a democratic socialist ethos at this most propitious moment in British history can be seen as a lost opportunity. As McKibbin (1998) notes:

Anyone who visited England in 1939 and then in 1950 would have been astonished at the political transformation. The extraordinary hegemony of the Conservative Party had been overthrown quite unexpectedly and in its stead a Labour government had carried through a programme of social welfare and nationalization which would have seemed impossible in 1939. But the visitor would have found the institutions of civil society almost wholly recognizable and the old 'ideological apparatus of the state' largely intact. Outside the realm of social services or nationalized industries the visitor would not have observed a social democracy.

(p. 536)

For Marxist commentators, such as Miliband (1961) and Saville (1977), the difficulties that Labour faced in trying to create a democratic socialist society owed more to their rigid adherence to a parliamentary road to change and an over-optimistic view of the benevolent potential of state action. For these critics, Labour's commitment to the national interest, rather than the class interests of its key supporters, and its reluctance to embrace extra parliamentary action meant that it would remain a party of social reform not socialism.

From another perspective, Labour's failure to pursue a more radical policy agenda can better be explained by the public's seemingly limited appetite for socialism (Black 2003a,b). Certainly, many within the party, not least Morrison, were optimistic that the more selfless public attitudes displayed during wartime would continue into peacetime, particularly if the government took active steps to ensure that the social divisions of the past did not re-emerge. Accordingly, new classless housing schemes were designed in ways that would foster a strong sense of community. Citizens were also encouraged to participate in Joint Production Committees at their place of work and become active in their local communities. However, the results proved disappointing. As Fielding et al. (1995) concluded:

It became clear that many people were not really in sympathy with what Labour was trying to achieve. Britain might have come together to a certain extent during the war, but in the later 1940s had reverted to being a much divided society. Class and gender differences were pronounced, as were those based on occupation, place of residence and notions of respectability. In these circumstances, the impulse to community remained weak. Labour was struggling against the grain.

(p. 128)

Consolidation rules?

Labour's uncertainty about the next stage of the democratic socialist project provided support for those advocating a period of consolidation. From around 1947, Morrison was one of those calling for 'a halt – not necessarily a permanent one – to further measures towards planning or socialism' (Morgan 1992: 71). Consolidation was deemed necessary for a number of reasons. First, it was believed that there was little to be gained either economically or politically for pressing ahead with more extensive forms of public ownership on grounds of socialist principle. It was accepted that nationalization had not proved particularly popular and that the public would need to be persuaded of the value of such measures on a case by case basis. Secondly, given the raft of social legislation that had been introduced, there was no immediate need for further advance in the area of social policy. Thirdly, while citizens had accepted the need for post-war controls, the cumulative impact of government imposed 'austerity measures such as rationing was giving rise to growing levels of public dissatisfaction, particularly amongst the middle classes (Brooke 1995: 116–20). Finally, it was believed that an emphasis on consolidation might prove advantageous in the prospective electoral battle with a revitalized Conservative Party.

Labour's second term 1950–51

Labour's 1950 General Election manifesto reflected the growing groundswell within the Party for a period of consolidation. Although proposals for the nationalization of the water industry, cement and sugar and the 'mutualization' of industrial insurance were included, these measures were justified on economic rather than socialist grounds. In social policy, new legislation was not deemed necessary but rather 'the wise development, through efficient and economical administration' of existing services (Labour Party 1950: 8). Consolidation of this kind was not, however, intended to signify that Labour had lost interest in the creation of a new social order. As the manifesto made clear:

> Socialism is not bread alone. Economic security and freedom from the enslaving material bonds of capitalism are not the final goals. They are means to the greater end – the evolution of a people more kindly,

intelligent, free, co-operative, enterprising and rich in culture. They are means to the greater end of the full and free development of every individual person. We in the Labour Party – men and women from all occupations and from every sphere of life – have set out to create a community that relies for its driving power on the release of all the finer constructive impulses of man.

(Labour Party 1950: 1)

Labour entered the 1950 General Election campaign in a reasonably confident mood. The Gallup polls published in the *News Chronicle* prior to the election indicated that Labour was now ahead of the Conservatives after being ten points behind their rivals in the previous November (Morgan 1984). In addition, 'Party organization and finance were in good shape, with individual membership continuing to increase from 487,000 in 1945 to 729,000 in 1949, and union-affiliated membership almost doubling to 4,946,000 over the same period. Its record at by-elections had been formidable, with only low swings to the Conservatives and no seats lost' (Thorpe 2001: 119).

The polls once again proved correct and Labour duly won the election. However, despite securing 46.1% of the votes cast (compared with 43.4% for the Conservatives), Labour's majority was cut to just five seats. Although the Party retained a strong level of support in working class constituencies particularly in the north and west of the country, it lost ground in 'middle class' suburban and rural constituencies, particularly in London and the Home Counties. Although 'Labour's traditional supporters had drawn comfort from full employment and the introduction of new welfare reforms, notably the health service, many more affluent voters were frustrated by continuing restrictions' (Jefferys 1992: 49). Labour's position had also been weakened as a result of the Representation of the People Act of 1949. It has been estimated that Labour lost 30 seats as a direct result of the redistribution of seats from declining inner city areas to an expanding suburbia in 1948–49 (Morgan 1984: 406).

The first six months of Attlee's second term proved relatively harmonious, not least on the economic front with strong export growth, a stable currency and a balance of payments surplus. The retention of two marginal seats in by-elections in West Dunbartonshire, and Brighouse and Spenborough also boosted Party morale (Morgan 1984: 411–12). The unity that had been a key feature of the first Attlee government continued. This unity began to unravel, however, following the outbreak of war in Korea in June 1950. It was not the initial decision of the Cabinet to side with the United States in resisting North Korean aggression that led to discord, but rather the subsequent decisions to authorize significant increases in defence expenditure.

In order to cement the 'special relationship' between Britain and the United States, a defence budget of £4700 million for the period from 1951 to

1954 was approved by the Cabinet in January 1951 (Brivati 1996). Given the size of this expenditure, Gaitskell (who had succeeded the ailing Cripps as Chancellor in the autumn of 1950; see Clarke 2002) sought significant cuts in domestic spending. In terms of NHS expenditure, Gaitskell proposed a ceiling of £392 million per annum, as well as the introduction of user charges for dentures, spectacles and prescriptions. Bevan, who was now Minister of Labour, strongly opposed the introduction of charges believing that they were unnecessary and would undermine the very ethos of the welfare state (Tomlinson 1997b). Attempts to broker some form of Cabinet agreement between Gaitskell and Bevan over this matter proved futile. Following Attlee's decision to support his Chancellor, Bevan resigned from the government along with two junior ministers, Harold Wilson and John Freeman.

Gaitskell's first and only budget speech in April 1951 proved highly significant in terms of the future direction of Labour's welfare strategy. It provided the clearest indication yet that Labour's commitment to the welfare state would, in future, be conditional, rather than absolute. The idea that welfare expenditure should take automatic precedence over other government concerns, such as rearmament, was abandoned. Gaitskell's success in introducing health charges was of great symbolic significance, heralding as it did the ascendancy of 'revisionist' thinking within the Labour Party.

The revenue raising measures contained in Gaitskell's budget did little to enhance Labour's popularity at this time. In addition to NHS charges, increases were announced in income, purchase and entertainment taxes. More significantly, 'rearmament' had adverse economic consequences particularly on export levels. By the summer of 1951, Britain was once more experiencing serious balance of payments problems, occasioned by a huge rise in the price of imports and capital outflows. In response the weekly ration of bacon, butter and cheese was reduced still further. As Morgan (1984) notes, the British public 'were now being faced with new and even more insupportable burdens' (p. 478).

Despite less than propitious circumstances (the Persian oil crisis and growing industrial unrest), Attlee decided to seek a fresh electoral mandate in 1951. In its General Election manifesto of 1951 Labour stressed that it remained the best choice for preserving world peace, for maintaining full employment and high production levels, and for bringing down the cost of living and building a fairer society (Labour Party 1951a). As in 1950, great emphasis was placed on Labour's record in office: 'To-day, after six years of Labour rule and in spite of post-war difficulties, the standard of living of the vast majority of our people is higher than ever it was in the days of Tory rule. Never have the old folk been better cared for. Never had we so happy and healthy a young generation as we see in Britain to-day' (reprinted in Dale 2000b: 78). It was recognized, however, that 'much more remains to be done in the redistribution of income and property to ensure that those who create the nation's wealth receive their just reward' (p. 77).

In contrast to the previous year the opinion polls now predicted, again correctly, a Conservative victory (Clarke 1996: 240). Nevertheless, it proved to be a close run contest. On an 83% turnout, Labour obtained a slightly higher proportion of the popular vote than the Conservatives (48.8–48%). However, this was insufficient to prevent the Conservatives from securing an overall majority of 17 seats on an overall swing of 1.1%. Although Labour continued to pile up votes in their urban, working-class strongholds, their middle-class support continued to decline as evidenced by their loss of key suburban marginals to the Conservatives in East Anglia and the South East.

Despite being defeated, Labour's better than anticipated performance led many Party stalwarts to anticipate a rapid return to office to continue the socialist advance once the electorate had been given a brief reminder of Conservative mismanagement. However, Conservative success in two subsequent General Elections led Labour to reconsider its democratic socialist strategy. Should it become a party of social reform rather than one seeking to transform society?

Conclusion

This chapter has focused on the Labour government's attempt to create a democratic socialist welfare state and society in the period from 1945 to 1951. Despite difficult economic circumstances Labour pursued a social and economic strategy that provided citizens with far greater protection from the five giants identified by Beveridge. The introduction of these services formed part of Labour's longer-term plan to establish a socialist commonwealth. By the end of the 1940s, however, the Labour government seemed less certain about the steps it needed to take in order to create a democratic socialist society. It appeared to have over-estimated the public's desire for change and to have under-estimated deep rooted commercial, institutional and cultural resistance to socialist ideas. While the call for a period of consolidation in such circumstances was understandable, it would only prove of lasting benefit if it led to a clearer articulation of Labour's future plans. As it was, these plans were to be developed in opposition rather than in government. The 'revisionist' strategy that eventually emerged is one of the themes of the next chapter which will focus on welfare developments in the age of 'consensus' from 1951 to 1979.

Further reading

Morgan (1984), Jefferys (1992), Hennessy (1993), Pearce (1994) and Brooke (1995) have provided scholarly reviews of the Attlee governments. Martin Francis' (1997) informative account of Labour's ideas and policies during this period is also to be recommended. Barnett (1986) and Dell (1999) provide more critical accounts of the Attlee years, while Tomlinson (1997a,b) has written authoritative overviews of the economic policies pursued by the Attlee administrations.

chapter

three

Revisiting the Welfare State from 1951–1979: an era of consensus in social policy?

The period between 1951 and 1979 has often been characterized as an era in which both Conservative (1951–64 and 1970–74) and Labour (1964–70 and 1974–79) governments came to accept the need for a mixed economy, the welfare state and economic interventionism in order to secure both growth and full employment. This so-called consensus between the two main parties even led *The Economist* to introduce its readers to a composite figure named Mr Butskell in 1954, in recognition of the difficulty in detecting any significant differences between the economic policies pursued by the then Conservative Chancellor R.A. Butler and his Labour predecessor Hugh Gaitskell (Kelly 2002). While this proved to be a highly influential journalistic innovation, the 'existence' of Mr Butskell has been questioned. As Gilmour and Garnett (1998) contend:

> Certainly both Gaitskell and Butler favoured Keynesian techniques and sought to maintain full employment. Both were moderates and both had good political manners. Both too had considerable respect for each other, but Gaitskell had (in Butler's words) 'unquenchably socialist' convictions and a strong belief in equality; Butler had no such convictions or belief. Moreover, he had in contrast to Gaitskell a belief in monetary policy and much less interest in planning. Butler favoured convertibility; Gaitskell defended exchange controls and the sterling area.
>
> (p. 75)

Other commentators have also questioned the existence of a post-war consensus (Pimlott 1988; Jones and Kandiah 1996). In the light of such scepticism, this chapter will revisit the question of whether the two major parties did reach an agreement about the role and purpose of the welfare state between 1945 and 1979? In examining this issue consideration will be given first to the definitional debate relating to consensus. This will be followed by a review of the Conservative approach to social policy between 1945 and 1964. To what extent did the Conservatives come to accept the welfare arrangements that Labour had put in place between 1945 and 1951? Attention will then switch to developments in Labour's thinking on the welfare state from 1951 to 1970. How did Labour's welfare policy develop, both in opposition and government, during this period? Did they continue with a democratic socialist welfare policy or did they begin to pursue a more moderate agenda that moved them closer to the Conservative Party? The penultimate section of the chapter will examine the period between 1970 and 1979. Was this the critical period in which both parties came to accept that fundamental reform of the welfare state was necessary? An assessment of whether there was a welfare consensus between 1951 and 1979 will be offered in the conclusion.

The definitional debate

In attempting to determine whether a political consensus of any kind emerged in the post-1945 period, it is important to be clear about how the term is to be employed (see Kavanagh 1992; Seldon 1994). Some commentators, for example, use the term consensus to refer to the *framework* and institutional structures within which political debate and activity takes place. Evidence for a consensus of this kind could include broad cross-party support for parliamentary democracy, the rule of law, the role of the monarchy and civil service neutrality (see Heffernan 2002).

For others, a consensus has been equated with agreement over policy, both broad and specific (see Beer 1965). The post-war 'acceptance' by both Labour and Conservative governments of the need for both public and private forms of ownership, and for state intervention to secure full employment and economic growth is often cited as an illustration of a broad policy consensus. The decision by Churchill's Conservative government to retain the NHS, which had been introduced by a previous Labour government, can similarly be seen as an example of a more specific policy accord. From this *policy* approach to consensus, greater weight tends to be placed on the actions of a political party when in government rather than the policy agenda they adhered to when in opposition or the commitments made in General Election manifestos (see Kavanagh and Morris 1994).

Consensus has also been explored from an *ideological* perspective (see Pimlott 1988). From this viewpoint, the fact that Labour and the Conservatives have, on occasions, adopted similar policies when in government should not, it is argued, be regarded as *de facto* evidence of a 'true' consensus. An incoming government might decide to continue with the policy agenda of the previous administration as a temporary expedient while it prepares an alternative strategy. Moreover, as Hickson (2004a) argues, policy convergence may not necessarily reflect an ideological accord. Similar policies might be pursued for very different ends. As was noted in Chapter One, for example, the fact that Labour and Conservative members of Churchill's coalition government agreed to certain welfare initiatives during the Second World War was not deemed sufficient to merit the ascription of a welfare consensus given that there was no shared vision about the role and purpose of these measures.

The fact that both the Conservative and Labour parties have continually emphasized their distinctive political values and standpoints, provides a good reason for examining the existence or otherwise of a post-war consensus on welfare from an *ideological* standpoint. Accordingly, the key question that will be addressed in this chapter is whether a political consensus was formed between Labour and the Conservatives in relation to the fundamental ethos of the welfare state in the post-1945 era.

When examining the post-war welfare consensus thesis, one further issue needs to be resolved, namely the period in which such an accord might be said to have operated (Dutton 1991; Kavanagh and Morris 1994). As Lowe (1990) points out, 'the conventional chronology is either May 1940–May 1979 (from the appointment of Churchill's Coalition government to the election of Mrs Thatcher) or June 1944–September 1976 (from the publication of the Employment Policy White Paper to Callaghan's renunciation of the commitment to full employment)' (p. 156). Others, however, have suggested alternative time frames. Marwick (2003) plumps for 1945–57, while Holmes opts for the period between 1972 and 1975 (see Lowe 1990: 156). Given that it has already been suggested in Chapter One that a welfare consensus did not emerge between 1940 and 1945, the period selected for review here will follow a modified version of Lowe's 'conventional chronology' starting with the election of the Attlee government in 1945 and concluding with the arrival of Margaret Thatcher in Downing Street in 1979.

Modern Conservatism (1945–64): a new approach to state welfare?

The scale of the Conservative Party's defeat in the 1945 General Election suggested that it had failed to persuade a majority of the electorate that it had developed a forward looking policy agenda (Kandiah 1995). Despite manifesto commitments to 'the maintenance of a high and stable level of employment' (Dale 2000a: 63) and the creation of 'a comprehensive health service covering the whole range of medical treatment from the general practitioner to the specialist' (p. 63), Conservatism continued to be associated more with appeasement, the defence of privilege and latent hostility to state intervention.

Electoral defeat in 1945 provided an opportunity for progressives within the Party to press for the adoption of a new image and outlook along the lines previously formulated by the Next Five Years Group (1935), by Macmillan in *The Middle Way* (1938) and by the Tory Reform Committee (which had been established in 1942). From this perspective, it was seen as imperative to convince the public that the Conservatives were now committed to a policy agenda that aimed to strike a better balance between individualism and collectivism as well as the market and the state.

In response to a resolution from delegates at the Party Conference in Blackpool in 1946 calling for a clearer statement of Conservative principles and aims, Churchill, who continued to lead the Party, appointed an industrial policy committee under the chairmanship of R.A. Butler. This resulted in what some have come to regard 'as one of the pivotal statements of postwar Conservatism' (Taylor 2002: 85; see also Ball 2003: 8) – *The Industrial Charter* (Conservative and Unionist Central Office 1947). While the Charter made clear that the Party remained committed to free enterprise and limited regulation of industry, it also sought to reassure sceptics that a future Conservative government would seek to establish positive relationships with the trade unions, whom they believed had much to contribute to 'the national welfare' (p. 21), and to take all necessary steps to 'ensure that the demand for goods and services is always maintained at a level which will offer jobs to all who are willing to work' (p. 16). In an effort to dispel the notion that a future Conservative administration would prioritize the rights of employers rather than employees, section III of *The Industrial Charter* was devoted to the concerns of workers. Under this section of the Charter, it was envisaged that employees should have 'a reasonable expectation of industrial security' (p. 29), improved education and training opportunities, and enhanced status in the workplace. Joint consultative committees were to be encouraged not least because they would provide an opportunity for 'the ideas of those who carry out the job to be brought before the management and ensure that they are fully discussed in a co-operative and frank spirit' (p. 33).

While *The Industrial Charter* confirmed that the Conservatives wanted to be perceived as 'interventionist' Tories rather than *laissez-faire* Liberals, the reform they were seeking did not amount to what one leading right wing MP, Sir Waldron Smithers, alleged was a faint hearted compromise 'with socialism and communism' (quoted in Dorey 2002: 141). As Addison (1992) observes, there was much to 'please the free enterprise lobby' in the Charter, including a pledge to cut direct taxation and reduce the number of civil servants. There was also a commitment to curb trade union powers. The Charter promised to restore 'three important features' of the 1927 Trade Disputes Act, which Labour had repealed: 'the ban on the affiliation of civil service unions to the Labour party, the prohibition of the closed shop in the public sector, and the principle of contracting-in to the political levy' (p. 394).

The pragmatic nature of the Conservative reappraisal at this time was confirmed with the more wide-ranging review of policy contained in *The Right Road for Britain* (Conservative and Unionist Central Office 1949), drafted by Quintin Hogg, whose influential book, *The Case for Conservatism*, had appeared two years earlier (1947). *The Right Road for Britain* was published in the run-up to the 1950 General Election as 'a broad and simple statement of . . . Conservative outlook and aims' (p. 5). It contrasted the Party's defence of individualism and freedom with Labour's preference for 'a uniform and standard society in which the best is levelled down and success is the target of envious attacks' (p. 7). Although a vigorous defence of free enterprise and market forces was mounted in *The Right Road*, this was accompanied by strong support for the trade union movement, who were deemed to have a vital role to play in 'the proper working of our economy and of our industrial life' (p. 24). *The Right Road* also insisted that Conservatives were fully supportive of the 'new Social Services' not least because of the Party's historic achievements in this sphere. 'We regard them as mainly our own handiwork. We shall endeavour faithfully to maintain the range and scope of these Services, and the rates of benefit' (p. 42). Although the aim of *The Right Road* was to reassure the public that the welfare state was safe in Conservative hands, there were indications that the Conservative approach to social policy would differ from Labour's. Concern was expressed, for example, about the growing cost of the NHS, 'the tendency to create enormous and unwieldy multilateral schools' (p. 44), and the 'shameful' levels of waste and extravagance to be found in the public sector (p. 42).

A distinctly Conservative approach to social and economic policy was certainly detectable in the Party's General Election manifesto of 1950 – *This is the Road* (Conservative and Unionist Central Office, 1950). The manifesto contained commitments to bolster parental choice in education, enhance the 'disregard' rules for pensioners and 'maintain and improve the health service' primarily by means of efficiency savings (reprinted in Dale 2000a: 86). Emphasis was given to the vital role the private sector would play in creating a property-owning democracy. Substantial savings in government expenditure were called for as were tax cuts and an end to nationalization.

The One Nation Group

Following the Conservatives' narrow election defeat in 1950, nine newly elected backbench MPs (including Iain Macleod, Enoch Powell, Angus Maude and Edward Heath) established what came to be known as the One Nation Group (ONG) (Walsha 2000, 2003). 'At their first meeting at the Political and Economic Planning (PEP) offices at 16 Queen Anne's Gate, Macleod informed the group that he had been asked to write a pamphlet on the social services for the Conservative Political Centre (CPC)'. Macleod's suggestion that the preparation of this pamphlet (which the CPC had requested be published before the 1950 Party conference) should be jointly undertaken by the One Nation Group (ONG) was readily agreed to (Seawright 2005: 74). According to Walsha (2000), the aim of this pamphlet, *One Nation. A Tory Approach to Social Problems* (Macleod and Maude 1950) 'was to provide a powerful case for a distinctly Conservative welfare policy, which its authors believed essential for the party to be able to best socialist social welfare provision in both philosophy and practice. It was an attempt to provide an underpinning rationale to the hitherto piecemeal nature of Conservative policy-making' (p. 191).

In attempting to develop a modern Conservative welfare policy, the contributors to the pamphlet were keen to counter any suggestion that they were merely seeking a pragmatic accord with Labour's approach. While the ONG acknowledged that social welfare could help to elevate the condition of the people, they were acutely aware of the need to ensure that such activity did not undermine the prospects for economic prosperity. While the ONG were full of praise for those men and women, such as Owen, Oastler, Nightingale, Dickens, Kingsley, Morris and Shaftesbury who had campaigned tirelessly against 'laisser-faire' (p. 12), they remained committed to 'competitive free enterprise' which they believed represented the best means of achieving the high levels of 'efficiency and flexibility' required to increase the 'country's wealth' (pp. 72–3). They were particularly concerned about the adverse impact of Labour's redistributionist policies, which they thought endangered 'the future well-being of even the poorest' (p. 18). Moreover, they made it clear that pensioners could not expect any increase in their pensions 'for many years' because of the inflationary consequences of diverting 'resources from capital investment to immediate consumption' (p. 63).

The ONG, then, was keen to establish a Conservative approach to social policy that was both distinctive and modern. According to one leading scholar of modern Conservatism, Robert Walsha (2000), the ONG had no wish to 'engineer or consolidate the case for a compromised form of Conservatism intent on meeting socialism part-way' (p. 190). As they made clear in the opening paragraph of *One Nation*:

> There is a fundamental disagreement between Conservatives and Socialists on the question of social policy. Socialists would give the same benefits to everyone, whether or not the help is needed, and indeed whether or not the country's resources are adequate. We believe that we must first help those in need. Socialists believe that the State should provide an average standard. We believe that it should provide a minimum standard, above which people should be free to rise as far as their industry, their thrift, their ability or their genius may take them.
>
> (Macleod and Maude 1950: 9)

The ONG believed, then, that the Conservatives should distance themselves from Labour by prioritizing economic stability above egalitarian social spending, selectivity over universalism and the pursuit of minimum, rather than optimal levels of state welfare provision.

Although the main focus of *One Nation* was to establish the broader parameters of a modern Conservative approach to welfare, the group were prepared to make some incursions into specific areas of policy. In housing, for example, the 're-creation of a large and expanded sector for private house-building' (p. 35) was seen as the key to increasing the supply of competitively priced homes for rent or purchase. The case for easing restrictive planning and licensing regulations was advanced as was the re-direction of local authority activity away from the needs of 'better off' tenants towards a focus on slum clearance and 'the abatement of overcrowding' (p. 36).

Improving primary schooling was the main educational priority. 'If the basic schooling given there is inadequate, or if the child's eagerness to learn is killed at the primary stage by dreary surroundings and uninspired or over-burdened teachers, money spent on secondary or further education is largely wasted' (p. 48). Attention was also drawn to the importance of improving technical schools and colleges and of introducing higher rates of pay for teaching staff.

While the need to improve some areas of health care was acknowledged in *One Nation*, the rising cost of provision, particularly in the dental service, was the issue of principal concern. Effective prioritization of need coupled with user charges were seen as the key to increasing revenue and curbing unnecessary demand. Moreover, 'any sentimental urge to divert, through state action, too great a proportion of the nation's resources to the old' was to be firmly resisted (p. 64). Informal care and voluntary action were seen as having a leading role to play in meeting the 'welfare' needs of older people.

Although *One Nation* accepted the case for pragmatic forms of welfare collectivism, this was not seen as involving any rejection of traditional Conservative concerns such as sound finance, efficiency, lower taxation, thrift, self-reliance, voluntarism and charitable activity (Walsha 2000). As Green (2002) makes clear, 'In spite of their Disraelian moniker, which carried the historical baggage of the nineteenth-century Tory critique of laissez faire, One Nation sought to blend judicious Statism with strong inflections of liberal market, laissez-faire ideas' (p. 247).

Subsequent One Nation publications serve to confirm this assessment. In *Change Is Our Ally* (Powell and Maude 1954) the recognition that 'social and political considerations should often override economic ones' did not 'invalidate the general principle that freely-operating competition is the most effective means of promoting economic advantage' (p. 96). Similarly, in *The Responsible Society* (One Nation Group 1959), it was made clear that modern Conservatives were not in favour of ever-increasing levels of state welfare provision. On the contrary, the Party remained 'predisposed (as most Socialists are not) to let the individual pay and act for himself when he can' (p. 35).

In essence, the modern approach to the welfare state that the Conservatives began to pursue from the late 1940s mirrored 'the traditional Conservative philosophy of conserving what is best in the old while adapting constantly to the new' (Lowe 2005: 25). While modern Conservatives remained committed to the market on the grounds that it provided 'the best practical mechanism for ensuring individual initiative and hence political freedom, economic efficiency and social justice' (p. 205), it was now recognized that some forms of state intervention in areas, such as welfare would complement, rather than undermine the progressive potential of the market. This acceptance of the need for state welfare provision was not, however, seen as signalling a conversion to Labour's transformative approach. As Glennerster (2007) points out, 'what emerged from this rethinking was not . . . a meek acceptance of the Welfare State as it was being created by Bevan and Griffiths. The cost, the way it was being financed, and the form it was taking were all offensive to the liberal view of the state that became the basis of Conservative philosophy. There should be some welfare provision, to be sure, but it should have a Conservative face' (p. 74).

While the Conservatives were keen to dispel the notion that they were ideologically opposed to the welfare state, they did not place undue emphasis on welfare issues in their electoral strategy in the early 1950s (Seldon 1981). Instead, they stressed their commitment to 'setting the people free' from stifling bureaucratic controls, rationing and shortages (see Zweiniger-Bargielowska 2000).

The Conservatives return to power

In his 1951 General Election address, Churchill argued that only a stable Conservative administration 'not biased by privilege or interest or cramped by doctrinal prejudices or inflamed by the passions of class warfare' would be able to foster enterprise, increase the availability of consumer goods, 'halt the rising cost of living', and 'prune waste and extravagance' in all government departments (*General Election Manifesto of the Conservative and Unionist Party of 1951*, reprinted in Dale 2000a: 95–9). The Conservative strategy of presenting itself 'as the champion of the female consumer by recognizing the burden borne by women under post-war austerity and promising relief in the form of decontrol, restoration of the price mechanism, and increased supplies of consumer goods' (Zweiniger-Bargielowska 2000: 262) proved highly effective in regaining the support of women voters in the 1951 General Election. The Conservatives also exploited popular dissatisfaction about the supply of housing by promising to build 300,000 new homes each year. As Jones (2000) notes, 'The perception of Labour failures in housing gave Conservative policy-makers the opportunity to showcase free enterprise, which they argued would provide more houses more quickly and more efficiently. The promise to build 300,000 houses a year was therefore seen within the party as central to the revival of popular support for market values in post-war Britain' (p. 117).

The depth of the Conservative commitment to the welfare state was quickly tested following their narrow election victory in 1951. Faced with a substantial balance of payments deficit that had triggered international speculation against the pound, Butler, the incoming Chancellor, opted to cut imports, tighten monetary policy and review public expenditure commitments (Boxer 1996). Although a number of cost containment measures were introduced, such as the introduction of NHS charges and a reduction in the school building programme (1952), Butler 'stood resolute against any attempt to commission another Geddes Axe – the exercise that had rapidly halted the expansion of welfare expenditure after the First World War' (Bridgen and Lowe 1998: 12–13). Indeed, once this economic turbulence had subsided following the end of the Korean War and the onset of more favourable terms of trade, modest expenditure increases in areas such as social security were introduced (Seldon 1981). Although there were no major realignments in social policy during what turned out to be Churchill's final term as Prime Minister, it would be mistaken to interpret this as a belated acceptance of Labour's egalitarian approach to the welfare state.

The appointment of more 'progressive' ministers in areas such as health (Macleod 1952–55) and education (Eccles 1954–57) served to strengthen the pro-welfare lobby in government. This did not signal, however, a declining interest in the desirability of sustaining a distinctly Conservative approach to the welfare state, involving as it did increased targeting, a greater reliance on charging and stricter expenditure controls (Raison 1990). Both the establishment of the Phillips Committee on the Economic and Financial Problems of Provision for Old Age (Cmd. 9333 1953) and the Guillebaud enquiry into the costs of the NHS (Cmd. 9663 1956) were indicative of an underlying desire to pursue a Conservative welfare agenda. There was a clear recognition, however, that the pace of such change should be gradual, rather than sudden, if the Party was to retain public support. Indeed, Butler's decision to authorize a review of NHS expenditure, rather than social service spending in general, which Macleod had been pressing for, was based on his fear that a wider ranging enquiry would revive public concerns about a Conservative desire to dismantle the welfare state (Glennerster 2007: 87).

By the time of the 1955 General Election the Conservatives, now under the leadership of Eden, were keen to emphasise their distinctive approach to the welfare state:

> We denounce the Labour Party's desire to use the social services, which we all helped to create, as an instrument for levelling down. We regard social security, not as a substitute for family thrift, but as a necessary

basis or supplement to it. We think of the National Health Service as a means, not of preventing anyone from paying anything for any service, but of ensuring that proper attention and treatment are denied to no one. We believe that equality of opportunity is to be achieved, not by sending every boy and girl to exactly the same kind of school, but by seeing that every child gets the schooling most suited to his or her aptitudes. We see a sensible housing policy in terms, not of one hopeless Council waiting list, but of adequate and appropriate provision both for letting and for sale.

> (*United for Peace and Progress, the Conservative and Unionist Party's General Election Manifesto* 1955, reprinted in Dale 2000a: 119)

Conservative pledges to maintain full employment, to double living standards within 25 years, to reduce taxes and to create a property-owning democracy appeared to resonate with the aspirations of an increasingly 'affluent' British public. The Conservatives recorded a comfortable electoral victory in May 1955 increasing their overall majority from 17 to 59 seats.

Modern Conservatism takes hold

The modern Conservative approach to social policy became firmly entrenched during both the Eden (1955–57) and Macmillan (1957–63) eras. Traditional Conservative 'economic' concerns, such as low taxes and price stability, were now to be balanced against 'social' imperatives, such as the need to maintain full employment and protect the welfare state. This gave rise to a number of policy dilemmas for Eden and Macmillan as they sought to maintain economic stability without resorting to price or wage controls, tax increases or reductions in social expenditure (Rollings 1996; Whiteside 1996). Treasury concern about the escalating cost of the welfare state did, however, lead to the establishment of a Cabinet committee on the Social Services, which held its first meeting under the chairmanship of Butler in 1956. Although Treasury officials outlined a range of policy options designed to restrain the growth of social expenditure, such as increased NHS charges, raising the school entry age to 6 and increasing the price of school meals, they were unable to persuade a majority of committee members of the need for such measures. Indeed, as Lowe (1989) points out, the committee's forensic dissection of Treasury claims about economically unsustainable increases in social expenditure and the positive impact that expenditure retrenchment would have on the rate of inflation, work incentives and 'foreign confidence in sterling' only served to strengthen the case for *maintaining* financial support for the welfare state not least because it often represented a form of investment rather than consumption (p. 515).

Arguably the most significant policy clash between modern and more traditionally minded Conservatives occurred in 1958 when the then Chancellor, Thorneycroft, demanded a sizeable cut in social spending in order to tackle inflationary pressures in the economy and restore international confidence in sterling. Although there was general agreement about the need to control expenditure, a number of Thorneycroft's specific proposals such as 'hospital boarding charges, the removal of the non-hospital ophthalmic service from the NHS and the withdrawal of family allowance from the second child' (p. 519) proved unacceptable to his Cabinet colleagues. Although cuts of £100 million, rather than the £153 million sought by Thorneycroft, were agreed, this was deemed inadequate by the Chancellor, who along with two of his junior Treasury ministers, Enoch Powell and Nigel Birch, resigned. Although this episode is often presented as evidence that 'social priorities had taken precedence over the curbing of inflation' (Morgan 1992: 175) in relation to Conservative policy making, such assessments should be treated with caution. Rollings (1996) maintains, for example, that this event should be viewed as a difference in economic policy making, rather than the prioritization of social policy: 'It is a caricature to depict the Thorneycroft resignation and the reflationary action of 1958 as the abandonment of the objectives of controlling inflation and maintaining confidence in sterling' (p. 113). It was more a difference of opinion over the precise measures needed to exercise inflationary control and maintain currency stability at a particular moment in time.

Macmillan's description of this event as a 'little local difficulty' proved apt at least in terms of subsequent political developments. A growing economy coupled with Amory's expansionary pre-election 'give-away' budget, in which the standard rate of income tax 'was cut from 43.5 to 38.75 percent; purchase tax was cut by a sixth; investment allowances were restored; and 2d was taken off a pint of beer' (Sandbrook 2005: 89), enabled Macmillan to secure a third consecutive election victory for the Conservatives in October 1959. The electorate seemed to be persuaded that the Conservatives had indeed succeeded in creating 'One Nation at home' through improvements in living standards and social reform (*The Next Five Years: The Manifesto of the Conservative and Unionist Party for the General Election 1959*, reprinted in Dale 2000a: 130).

This electoral popularity proved short-lived, as Macmillan had to grapple with a range of economic difficulties on the home front, as well as the French veto on Britain's application to join the Common Market and the Profumo affair in 1963 (Jefferys 2002).

A severe sterling crisis in 1961 led the government to request a loan from the International Monetary Fund, which was granted on condition of future public expenditure restraint (see Childs 2001: 100–1). Treasury attempts to secure the necessary economies again proved unsuccessful as those like Macmillan and Eccles who were committed to what Bridgen and Lowe (1998) term 'creative dirigisme', rather than '*laissez-faire*', continued to hold the upper hand. While Macmillan's decision to replace a third of his Cabinet in the 'Night of the Long Knives' in 1962 could be said to represent the emergence of ever-deeper conflict between traditional and modern Conservatives, it is important not to overstate this apparent division. Certainly, the modern Conservatives were not seeking to prioritize social imperatives over economic ones. Indeed, the Party's internal review of the Future of the Social Services (1961–63) again considered some highly contentious issues such as 'the withdrawal of the universal state pension and the charging of fees in state schools' (Bridgen and Lowe 1998: 11). However, these radical solutions to the growth of welfare spending were rejected on the grounds that current government policies, such as increased health and social security contributions and the move to economic rents for council house tenants, were based on a 'less confrontational' form of targeting (p. 11).

A re-spray or a refit?

Macmillan's resignation in 1963 has been regarded as halting the advance of modern Conservatism. Certainly, as will be seen in Chapter Four, the Thatcher administrations from 1979 to 1990 were, in comparison to the Macmillan governments, more hostile towards economic interventionism and the welfare state. Indeed, as Ritschel (1995) reminds us, some neo-liberal critics have come to regard modern Conservatism as 'a corrupt and debilitating compromise with socialism which diverted the party from the true Conservative path' (p. 66). While it is undoubtedly the case that modern Conservatism led to policy innovation, it is questionable whether this should be regarded as a departure from progressive forms of Toryism. Indeed, the flexible social and economic interventionism undertaken by modern Conservatives such as Macmillan during the 1950s and 1960s were merely the latest attempts to secure 'balanced economic development and the historic Tory priorities of social cohesion and harmony' (p. 66).

The focus here, though, is whether the advance of modern Conservatism contributed to the emergence of a welfare consensus between the two major Parties in the period from 1951 to 1979. In order to pursue this question it is now necessary to turn to the second 'ideological' development referred to earlier, namely, revisionist democratic socialism.

Revisionist Democratic Socialism 1951–70

As noted at the end of Chapter Two, there were already signs that the post-war Labour government was beginning to rethink its economic and social strategy by the time of the 1951 General Election. In terms of the former, there was greater support for the notion that capitalism needed to be controlled or managed by fiscal and monetary means rather than abolished (Tomlinson 1997a). It was also recognized that the initial phase of public ownership had not transformed employer-employee relationships or given rise to 'much interest, excitement, or loyalty' amongst the wider public (Brooke 1995: 20). Indeed, a more muted approach to public ownership could be detected in the Party's General Election manifesto of 1951 when the specific commitments contained in the 1950 address were omitted in favour of a modest pledge to nationalize private industries 'which fail the nation' (Thorpe 2001: 123). In the case of its social strategy, Labour reaffirmed its commitment to the creation of a more equal society through such measures as full employment and the welfare state:

> Contrast Britain in the inter-war years with Britain today. Then we had mass unemployment; mass fear; mass misery. Now we have full employment. Then millions suffered from insecurity and want. Now we have social security for every man, woman and child. Then dread of doctors' bills was a nightmare in countless homes so that good health cost more than most people could afford to pay. Now we have a national health scheme which is the admiration of the post-war world. Then we had the workhouse and the Poor Law for the old people. Now we have a national insurance system covering the whole population with greatly improved pensions and a humane National Assistance scheme.
>
> (*Labour Party General Election Manifesto of 1951*, reproduced in Dale 2000b: 77)

It was acknowledged, though, that more needed to be done to eliminate poverty and ensure a fairer distribution of income and wealth.

The 1951 manifesto provided few clues, however, as to how Labour's broader objective of social transformation was to be achieved. It merely promised to 'press forward towards greater social equality and the establishment of equal opportunities for all' (pp. 77–8). The absence of a more explicit strategy reflected the emergence of two contrasting approaches on the way forward within Labour circles. The narrowness of Labour's defeat in the 1951 General Election led the fundamental wing of the Party to press for the continuation of the interventionist economic and social strategy that Labour had been pursuing in government since 1945 (Jones 1996). Writing in 1952, Aneurin Bevan, for example, was adamant that the Party should accelerate its nationalization programme in order to ensure the relationship between 'public and private property was drastically altered' in favour of the former (see Bevan 1978: 118–19). While it was accepted that peacetime conditions necessitated some modifications in spheres such as food subsidies, price controls, production directives and wage restraint, any major reverse of socialist policy was to be firmly resisted.

In contrast, 'consolidators' such as Morrison believed that a more cautious approach should be taken. They argued that a thorough going assessment of the effectiveness of the first wave of nationalizations should be undertaken before further initiatives were pursued (see Donoughue and Jones 2001: chapter 33).

The more significant challenge to 'fundamentalism' came from younger revisionist thinkers within the Party such as Crosland and Jenkins (Crossman 1952). These thinkers were convinced that Labour needed to refresh its message especially if it was to counter Conservative claims, resonating with women voters in particular, that the restoration of free markets would obviate the need for peacetime austerity measures (see Zweiniger-Bargielowska 2000).

Crosland and the case for revisionism

Anthony Crosland's book *The Future of Socialism* (1956) quickly became seen as the key revisionist text within Labour circles. Crosland argued that post-war Britain was no longer the 'unreconstructed capitalist society' that it had been in 1939 (p. 57). Capitalist power and control had been diluted by the steady advance of democracy, increasing degrees of state intervention, growing trade union influence and the emergence of a more autonomous, socially responsive managerial class. These developments led Crosland to argue that different *means* now needed to be employed to create a more egalitarian society. Crucially, and most controversially, Crosland believed that more extensive public ownership was not necessary for the creation of a more egalitarian post-war society. 'State ownership of all industrial capital is not now a condition of creating a socialist society, establishing social equality, increasing social welfare, or eliminating class distinctions' (p. 497). Moreover, although Crosland acknowledged that further forms of economic equality were required, especially in the distribution of wealth, he contended that modern socialism should focus on social equality. 'The socialist seeks a distribution of rewards, status, and privileges egalitarian enough to minimize social resentment, to secure justice between individuals, and to equalize opportunities; and he seeks to weaken the existing deep-seated class stratification, with its concomitant feelings of envy and inferiority, and its barriers to uninhibited mingling between the classes' (p. 113). High quality forms of state provision in health care, housing and 'socially unifying' comprehensive schools (Harris 2000: 35) were seen as vital components of Crosland's strategy of equality.

Crosland gave primacy to social, rather than economic, equality on the grounds that any further redistribution of income would have limited impact on the well-being of the poor and would do little to tackle 'family-cultural disadvantage, which could only be addressed through state-provided services (particularly in education)'. Crucially, Crosland believed that egalitarian forms of social expenditure would prove more popular with middle-class taxpayers, who might derive some personal benefit from enhanced welfare provision, than through further redistribution of income which might engender greater resentment (p. 127). For Crosland, the attainment of socialism was best achieved by mechanical rather than moral means (see Clarke 1978). Unlike the moral reformer who seeks to create an egalitarian society by persuading higher income groups of their ethical 'duty' to support their less advantaged neighbours, the mechanical reformer believes that there are 'political, social and economic strategies available which would produce the desired results, without necessarily having to transform the underlying moral culture of citizens' (Plant 2002: 128–9). Crucially, though, Crosland's 'mechanical' welfare strategy was dependent on sustained economic growth that would provide 'a fiscal dividend for government to invest in public services'. This would have an 'egalitarian effect (at least in terms of social if not income inequality)' and would 'allow the absolute position of the better-off to be sustained while incrementally improving the relative position of the worst-off' (p. 130).

Not surprisingly, Crosland's revisionist 'turn' with its optimistic assumptions about the transformed nature of capitalism found little favour with fundamentalists, who believed that the contemporary form of this economic system remained 'unjust and inefficient' as well as 'immoral and ugly' (Cronin 2004: 55). The fundamentalists were concerned that the revisionists were less committed to achieving major change in British society. Certainly, such concerns seemed to be justified by Crosland's declaration in *The Future of Socialism* that he did not 'want to see *all* private education disappear: nor the Prime Minister denied an official car, as in one Scandinavian country: nor the Queen riding a bicycle: nor the House of Lords instantly abolished: nor the manufacture of Rolls-Royces banned: nor the Brigade of Guards, nor Oxford and Cambridge . . . lose their present distinctive character' (Crosland 1956: 217). The fundamentalists also questioned the revisionists' emphasis on individual, rather than collective well-being. Certainly, Crosland believed that a more affluent and consumerist public wanted to break free from the constraints of austerity and rectitude (see Black 2003a,b). For Crosland it was now time 'for a greater emphasis on private life, on freedom and dissent, on culture, beauty, leisure, and even frivolity. Total abstinence and a good filing-system are not now the right sign-posts to the Socialist utopia' (Crosland 1956: 524).

Revisionism takes hold

Labour's third consecutive electoral defeat in 1959 convinced the new Labour leader Hugh Gaitskell (who had succeeded Attlee in 1955) that Labour was losing touch with 'swing voters' (Wring 2005). In response to this setback, Gaitskell pursued a more explicitly revisionist political strategy including a controversial, and ultimately unsuccessful, attempt to redraft Clause Four of the Party's constitution (which related to public ownership) in an effort to reassure an apparently sceptical electorate that Labour's commitment to nationalisation was selective and strategic rather than doctrinaire (see Jones 1996: chapter 4).

The debate about 'Clause Four' only served to highlight the continuing division between the fundamentalist and revisionist wings of the Party. There were signs, though, that this rift was finally beginning to heal at the beginning of the 1960s. According to Pimlott (1992), two key Party publications, *Labour in the Sixties* (Labour Party 1960) and *Signposts for the Sixties* (Labour Party 1961) served to bridge 'the gap between right and centre-left and demonstrated the lack of distance between them' (p. 272). These documents made it clear that the Party's continued support for the mixed economy was now to be combined with a growth oriented scientific revolution that would necessitate increased reliance on both public ownership and planning.

This emphasis on scientific and technological change intensified under Harold Wilson, who was elected as Labour's leader following Gaitskell's sudden death in 1963. As Jones (1996) notes, Wilson's insistence that 'a future Labour government would ensure that new developments in science and technology would be introduced in a purposeful way through economic planning rather than through the haphazard interplay of unregulated market forces' served 'to redefine Labour's socialist purpose in contemporary terms' (p. 77). Importantly, this strategy also enabled Labour to reach out to aspiring middle-class voters, such as 'scientists, technicians, managers and skilled workers – whose advance was held to be blocked by a privileged, complacent and amateurish Establishment' (p. 78).

Wilson embraced the growth led revisionist welfare strategy outlined by Crosland. As the Party's General Election manifesto of 1964, *Let's Go with Labour for the New Britain*, made clear:

> Drastic reforms are now needed in our major social services. To make them fit for the 1960s and 70s will be costly in money, manpower and resources. This will not be achieved all at once: but, as economic expansion increases our national wealth we shall see to it that the needs of the community are increasingly met. *For the children*, this will mean better education; *for the family* decent houses at prices that people can afford; *for the sick*, the care of a modernized health service; *for the old people and widows*, a guaranteed share in rising national prosperity.
>
> (Labour Party 1964: 13)

A number of specific welfare pledges were put forward. In education, Labour promised to reduce class sizes, reorganize secondary education 'on comprehensive lines', increase the school leaving age to 16 and oversee a 'massive expansion in higher, further and university education' (pp. 13–14). Labour also vowed to 'reconstruct the social security system' by increasing National Insurance benefits (and subsequently linking them with the rise in average earnings) and introducing a non-stigmatized Income Guarantee for pensioners and widows.

In health care, prescription charges were to be abolished as a first step towards the restoration of 'a completely free Health Service' (p. 17). A properly funded hospital plan was to be put in place and the numbers of qualified medical staff increased.

Labour's narrow victory in the 1964 General Election followed by a more impressive success in 1966 provided an opportunity for the Party to pursue its ambitious welfare agenda. Once in government, however, Labour was confronted with serious economic difficulties. It proved difficult to stimulate growth and investment, maintain the value of sterling, avoid deflation, control wages, modernize the economy, avoid 'stop-go' economic policies (Tomlinson 2004a) and retain international confidence in the harsher climate of the time. Moreover, various 'white heat' innovations, such as the Department of Economic Affairs and the Ministry of Technology failed to ignite the economy (Jones 1996; Sandbrook 2006).

Ultimately, Labour's attempt to combine economic efficiency and social justice was blown off course by a succession of economic crises culminating in the humiliating currency devaluation of 1967. Although the economic situation improved markedly during the final years of the 1964–70 government, many Labour supporters were disillusioned by government decisions to withdraw proposed increases in social security benefits, postpone the raising of the school leaving age and reimpose prescription charges.

Reversals of this kind served to intensify the concerns that some influential Labour sympathizers, such as the so-called 'Titmuss group' (Ellison 1994) at the London School of Economics had begun to express about the limited egalitarian impact of Labour's welfarism (Abel-Smith 1958; Townsend 1958; Abel-Smith and Townsend 1965). Indeed, by the time of the General Election campaign of 1970, the Wilson government was battling to refute the charge made by the Child Poverty Action Group that the position of the poor had actually worsened under Labour (McCarthy 1986; see Tomlinson 2004a, on the validity of this claim).

Given that Labour's ambitious plans for social policy were now premised on economic growth, it was inevitable that failure to achieve this latter objective would have an adverse effect on the former. The severity of the economic circumstances confronting Labour at this time prompts Thorpe (2001) to suggest, however, that we should 'be more surprised at what the government was able to do, than condemnatory of what it failed to achieve in social policy' (p. 154). Certainly, the extent of Labour's achievements in this era should not be ignored (see Tomlinson 2004b: Hills and Stewart 2005b). In the case of social security, less stigmatizing benefit procedures were introduced as part of a move to a 'rights-based' service. National Insurance benefit levels were increased, the earnings rule for widows was abolished and earnings-related unemployment and sickness benefits were introduced. Significant progress was made in the area of comprehensive secondary education following the request from the Department of Education for local authorities to submit plans for the development of non-selective schooling. As Timmins (2001) notes, 'by 1970 the proportion of pupils in schools that at least in name were comprehensive had risen from 10 to 32 per cent, and by the time Labour left office only eight authorities were actively refusing to submit plans' (p. 242).

The Wilson years had also seen a concerted attempt to extent personal liberty in areas such as penal reform, homosexuality, divorce, censorship and capital punishment. Although a number of these measures came onto the statute book as a result of Private Members' Bills, few would gainsay Marquand's (2004) assessment that 'the courageous and buoyant liberalism' of Home Secretary Roy Jenkins (1965–67) was decisive in smoothing the passage of what proved to be highly controversial legislation. Labour also sought to improve 'race relations' through the introduction of legislation in 1965 and 1968, and the establishment of the Community Relations Commission in 1968. However, its 'two-pronged policy' (Marwick 2003: 133) under which increased protection for migrants who were legally settled in Britain was counter-balanced by restrictions on those seeking residence (such as the Commonwealth Immigrants Act of 1968, which was rushed through to prevent the sizeable migration of the Asian community from East Africa) proved contentious (see Foot 1965; Glennerster 2007: 146–9).

Despite its many achievements it is difficult, on reflection, to take issue with Ellison's (1994) assessment that 'the abiding image of the 1964–70 Labour government was 'of a party beset by criticism from within and without, in many ways doing its best to maintain the welfare state that it had created but, owing to constant economic difficulties, failing to live up to the egalitarian hopes of its supporters' (p. 435). The 1970s, as we shall see below, proved no less troubling.

A 'consensus' of doubt: modern Conservatism, revisionist Democratic Socialism and the Welfare State in the 1970s

In the increasingly turbulent economic and social climate of the 1970s (O'Connor 1973) the 'commitment' of both the modern Conservatives and Labour's revisionist democratic socialists towards the welfare state was put to the test. The prevailing Conservative approach towards the welfare state was being challenged by neo-liberal critics suggesting that provision of this kind was undermining the economic and social fabric of the nation. The revisionist democratic socialists were facing criticisms that the level of welfare provision was inadequate and failing to have an impact on the inequality. Let us look at each of these challenges in turn.

The Neo-liberal challenge to modern Conservatism?
The Conservatives and the Welfare State: 1970–74

Although modern Conservatism was in the ascendancy in the post-war period, there were still those who remained committed to the Party's anti-collectivist tradition.

As was noted in Chapter One, for example, the Party chairman Ralph Assheton had promoted Hayek's book *The Road to Serfdom* (1944) during the General Election campaign of 1945. Although his effort to republish an abridged version of this text by Geoffrey Rippon for use during the election period proved in vain, the book did capture the imagination of some younger Conservative MPs such as Richard Law, whose influential book *Return from Utopia* (1950) 'urged the Party to turn its back on the Keynesian–Beveridgean Utopia' (pp. 98–9).

The establishment of the Institute of Economic Affairs (IEA) in 1955 proved to be particularly significant for the promotion of liberal Conservative ideas. The IEA attempted to persuade leading opinion formers in politics, higher education, business and the media of the merits of economic liberalism. In pursuit of this objective, the IEA published a series of pamphlets and research papers on topical issues such as state pensions (Seldon 1957), the financing of education (Peacock and Wiseman 1964) and choice in health care (Lees 1961). Over time, a number of influential Conservative politicians, such as Enoch Powell, Geoffrey Howe and Keith Joseph became increasingly persuaded of the merits of reshaping Conservative economic and social policy along neo-liberal lines.

Following two consecutive election defeats in 1964 and 1966, the Conservative Party started to give serious consideration to many of the ideas emanating from the IEA. At a pre-election conference held at the Selsdon Park Hotel in January 1970, the Party, now under the leadership of Edward Heath, considered a range of free market policies including tax cuts, curbs on trade union powers, reduced government support for failing industries and the ending of prices and incomes policies. In terms of the welfare agenda, the need for greater selectivity was emphasized, as were charges for the board and lodging components of an NHS hospital stay. This embrace of liberal ideas was seized upon by the Labour leader Harold Wilson who coined the phrase 'Selsdon man' to portray the Conservatives as the hard-hearted enemies of full employment, the welfare state and economic interventionism (although see Raison 1990, on this issue).

The Party's General Election manifesto of 1970 – *A Better Tomorrow* – was infused with a 'neo-liberal' ethos. As Blake (1998) notes, the manifesto committed the Party to 'libertarianism, lower direct taxation, reduction of trade union power, support for law and order . . . and minimal state intervention in industry' (p. 312). Indeed, for Willetts (1992) the preponderance of neo-liberal ideas in the 1970 manifesto leads him to conclude that it was 'more Thatcherite than the 1983 manifesto – and probably even the manifesto of 1979' (p. 42).

After the Conservative's unexpected victory in the General Election of 1970 (which some uncharitable commentators have even linked to 'blunders' by England's reserve goalkeeper Peter Bonetti that resulted in a quarter final defeat at the hands of West Germany in the World Cup tournament in Mexico; see Clarke 1996; Sandbrook 2006: 733–5), the new Heath government pushed ahead with a 'Selsdon' style policy agenda. Income and corporation tax were cut in Chancellor Barber's mini budget in October 1970; the incoming Minister of Trade and Industry, John Davies (the erstwhile Chair of the Confederation of British Industry), declared that taxpayers' money would no longer be used to bail out 'lame duck' industries; and industrial relations legislation (which proved inoperable in practice; Jefferys 2002) was to be brought forward in order to curb trade union power through the prohibition of closed shops, and by the enforcement of secret strike ballots and cooling-off periods.

This 'Selsdon' period proved to be short lived. Serious inflationary pressures (fuelled in part by Barber's expansionary budget), rising unemployment, bankruptcy at Rolls-Royce and the threatened closure of the Upper Clyde Shipbuilders led to a speedy return to interventionism. As Morgan (1992) notes, 'by mid-1971, Selsdon man had been decently interred and the government's policy went into rapid reverse' (p. 322).

By the end of 1972 wage controls were in place and a new Industry Act had been introduced which provided the government with powers to inject public money into the private sector when necessary. Although economic issues dominated the agenda of the Heath government, not least the two miners' strikes of 1972 and 1973 (leading, in the case of the latter, to a snap General Election in February 1974 over the question of 'who runs Britain?'; Jefferys 2002), there were a number of significant developments in the area of social policy.

Despite the Selsdon rhetoric in the Party's manifesto of 1970, the welfare policies pursued by the Heath government represented continuity with, rather than a radical departure from, the approach adopted by earlier post-war Conservative administrations (Raison 1990). Efforts were made, for example, to introduce judicious forms of selectivity in the areas of social security and housing. One notable innovation in terms of the former was the introduction of Family Income Supplement in 1973, a means-tested benefit designed to provide financial assistance for low-paid workers with dependent children (Hill 1993). The acceptance that state funding in areas such as health and education was compatible with modern Conservatism also ensured a continued commitment to expenditure in these areas. A White Paper entitled *Education: A Framework for Expansion* (Cmnd. 5174 1972) introduced by the education minister Margaret Thatcher in 1972 contained, for example, a commitment to increase teacher numbers by 40% within

10 years in order to lower the staff–pupil ratio: a pledge to ensure that 'half of all three-year-olds and 90 per cent of four-year-olds' would be entitled to a free, part-time nursery place by 1981: and a 60% rise in the number of higher education students over the same period (Timmins 2001: 300).

In his first party conference speech since becoming Prime Minister in June 1970, Heath referred to his desire to bring about 'a revolution so quiet and so total that it will go far beyond the programme of a Parliament' (quoted in Blake 1998: 309).

In practice, there was no fundamental change of this kind. Although Heath demonstrated a willingness to adjust economic and social policy in response to broader economic and social changes, there is little to suggest that his government's approach to economic interventionism or the welfare state differed fundamentally from the administrations of Churchill, Eden, Macmillan or Douglas-Home. As Gladstone (1999) notes, 'it was not until after the failure of the Heath government in 1974 that the so-called "New Right" began to win supporters on a large scale and to shape the rhetoric and ultimately the policies' of late-twentieth-century Conservatism (p. 55).

The flickering flame: Democratic Socialism and the Welfare State 1974–79

Labour's defeat in the 1970 General Election led to renewed questioning within the Party about the shortcomings of the revisionist strategy of the Wilson government. In particular, concerns were raised about the extent to which government could exercise influence in an era marked by the growth of global commerce and the rise of multi-national corporations (see Holland 1975). It was now recognized, as Tomlinson (2000) observes, that 'the private sector of the economy was no longer responsive to persuasion and incentives offered by government, and that a major extension of public ownership into the private manufacturing sector was required if a reforming government was to deliver its economic policy objectives' (p. 63). The establishment of a National Enterprise Board, which would take a stake in some of Britain's leading companies, was seen as a key way of re-establishing government influence in the economic sphere. The need for a new concordat with the trade unions was also acknowledged given the rising level of industrial unrest and the failure of Labour's last attempt to secure reform in this area (see Shaw 1996). A Social Contract was proposed that would commit the trade unions to wage restraint in exchange for government assurances that full employment policies would be pursued, high levels of public spending maintained and Conservative industrial relations legislation repealed.

There was less concern about the underlying approach that the 1964–70 Wilson governments had taken in relation to social policy. While it was recognized that there had been shortcomings in terms of delivery, this was attributed to adverse economic circumstances rather than any reluctance to pursue egalitarian policies. It was envisaged that the revitalized economic strategy would lead to the sustained levels of growth needed to fund egalitarian welfare provision.

Labour's General Election manifesto of February 1974 appeared to signal a return to a more 'fundamentalist' economic strategy promising as it did to 'bring about a fundamental and irreversible shift in the balance of power and wealth in favour of working people and their families' (Labour Party 1974). However, following their narrow victory, Wilson's minority government was unwilling to adopt the radical economic programme favoured in particular by the new Industry Secretary, Tony Benn (who was moved to the Department of Energy in 1975) and his deputy Eric Heffer. Indeed, both Wilson (1974–76) and Callaghan (1976–79) were unable even to pursue the more moderate revisionist socialist approach they favoured. Economic problems such as low growth, high inflation and rising unemployment continued to dominate the political agenda. As early as the spring of 1975 the Chancellor, Dennis Healey, was seeking Cabinet approval for social expenditure cuts in order to stabilize the economy. Further cuts were agreed by the Cabinet in 1976 as part of an International Monetary Fund (IMF) rescue package (Thorpe 2001).

Given the revisionist socialist doctrine that additional social expenditure was 'growth-dependent', this was a bleak era for social policy (Toynbee and Walker 2004). There were, nonetheless, a number of progressive initiatives. Public subsidies of private welfare were curbed by the decision to abolish the direct grant schools in 1975 and by the gradual phasing out of pay beds in NHS hospitals. Social security benefits (except for those in receipt of unemployment payments) were to be tied to the annual growth in prices or earnings (whichever was higher) and a State earnings-related pension scheme (SERPS) based on an individual's best 20 years of earnings was unveiled in 1975. The Housing (Homeless Persons) Act of 1977 enhanced the rights of vulnerable groups, such as lone parents and victims of domestic violence seeking council accommodation.

Persistent economic difficulties during this period led to more wide-ranging critiques of Keynesianism and to suggestions that the welfare state was approaching a crisis point (O'Connor 1973). As Tomlinson (2004b) observes:

> The mid-1970s are commonly seen as a watershed in post-war economic policy. The 'golden age' of the 1950s and 1960s came to an end in a period of 'stagflation' and crises over public spending, borrowing and the exchange rate. The 'Keynesian' consensus about how to conduct economic policy was fundamentally challenged by the sharp rise in both inflation and unemployment coupled to a major loss of financial confidence.
>
> (p. 55)

The Labour government's decision to prioritize the fight against inflation even if it resulted in higher levels of unemployment has been viewed by many leading commentators as a decisive retreat from Keynesianism (Dell 1999: 462: Glennerster 2007; see Tomlinson 2004b: 67).

Greater credence was also being given to the notion that the rising cost of the welfare state might be having an adverse impact on Britain's economic performance (see Bacon and Eltis 1976; Hickson 2004b). It was not just the rising cost of social expenditure that was seen as problematic, but also the 'rationale' for such spending. In the case of state education, for example, it was suggested that too great an emphasis was being placed on the inculcation of citizenship values rather than on employment driven competencies and skills that were more likely to have a beneficial impact on future economic prosperity (Lowe 2004b).

When a General Election was called in 1979 there were few (not least Callaghan himself; see Donoughue 2003) who thought that Labour would cling to power. As Seldon and Hickson (2004b) note, the 1974–79 Labour government had been 'attacked for mishandling of the economy, symbolized by the 1976 IMF crisis, for its failure to manage relations with the trade unions, culminating in the "winter of discontent" and for its failure to implement major changes in social policy' (p. 1). In contrast, the Conservatives under the new leadership of Margaret Thatcher were now viewed by the electorate as potential saviours of the nation with their heady combination of strong government and free markets (Gamble 1988).

The Welfare State 1951–79: an era of consensus?

The durability of Labour's post-war welfare edifice from 1951 to 1979 lends powerful support to the contention that this era can be described as one in which a consensus on social policy took root. The Conservatives did not attempt to abolish the National Health Service nor did they make major reforms to the social security system they inherited from Labour. The emergence of modern Conservatism heralded a rapprochement with the institutional welfare state and 'Keynesian' forms of economic interventionism (Lowe 1996). Significantly, though, this did not mean that the Conservatives had abandoned their belief in the need for differential rewards, the virtues of the free market, limited state intervention, voluntarism or self help. Instead economic intervention and basic state welfare provision were now seen as compatible with traditional Conservative beliefs (Willetts 1992).

This growing 'agreement' about means should not, however, be taken to indicate the emergence of an ideological convergence (Pimlott 1988) regarding the role and purpose of the welfare state. As Crosland observed in the early 1960s, 'no one supposes that the Conservatives will now suddenly dismantle the Welfare State, or utterly neglect the claims of the socially under-privileged groups. However, equally one can hardly deny that a deep difference exists between the two parties about the priority to be accorded to social welfare. This is not because Conservatives are necessarily less humanitarian, but because they hold particular views as to the proper role of the state, the desired level of taxation, and the importance of private as opposed to collective responsibility. Their willingness for social expenditure is circumscribed by these views; and the consequence is a quite different order of priorities' (Crosland 1962: 123). One crucial difference relates to the egalitarian role of the welfare state. While One Nation Conservatives rejected any form of equality 'beyond a minimalist conception of equality of opportunity', the revisionist socialists favoured 'a more thoroughgoing social and economic equality' (Hickson 2004a: 153).

Although Labour remained committed to creating an egalitarian welfare state, this objective proved more difficult to achieve following the adoption of the revisionist doctrine that progress in this sphere was dependent on economic growth. In an increasingly global economic environment, Labour found that it had fewer economic controls at its disposal and, as a consequence, could not achieve the growth rates needed for social advance. In addition, popular support for egalitarianism seemed to be in decline as a result of broader economic and social changes, such as subtle shifts in working class identity, the changing role of women in the home and workplaces, the impact of black immigration and attitudinal cleavages between the young and the old (Fielding 2003b). As Labour grappled with such changes, their ideological differences with the Conservatives were more observable at the level of theory, rather than in practical policy making.

Finally, while it is concluded here that there was *not* an ideological welfare consensus between the Conservatives and Labour in the period from 1951 to 1979, this does not rule out the possibility of such a convergence in the future. This would require, however, a change in underlying values, rather than policy adjustments. The perennial difficulty of course is deciding when a policy change is of such significance that it should be regarded as an indicator of a value shift. This issue needs to be kept in mind as our attention turns to the Conservative approach to the welfare state under the Thatcher and Major governments in Chapter Four and to New Labour in Chapter Five.

Further reading

The question of whether a consensus emerged between the Conservative and Labour governments during the post-1945 period has been addressed by a number of scholars including Beer (1965), Pimlott (1988), Dutton (1991), Kavanagh (1992), Sullivan (1992), Seldon (1994), Jones and Kandiah (1996), Heffernan (2002) and Hickson (2004b). Informative accounts of the theory and practice of Conservative social policy during the period from 1945 to 1979 are to be found in Raison (1990),

Jefferys (1997), Bridgen and Lowe (1998) and Hickson (2005). Labour's social strategy over the same period is reviewed in Morgan (1992), Ellison (1994), Fielding (1997), Diamond (2004), Plant *et al.* (2004) and Seldon and Hickson (2004a,b). Tony Crosland's (1956) *The Future of Socialism*, which was republished by Constable in 2006, remains the classic post-war revisionist Labour text.

chapter

four

Revisiting the Conservative welfare 'revolution': the Thatcher and Major years 1979–1997

This chapter will explore the Conservative approach to the welfare state during their period in government from 1979 to 1997. This era has come to be regarded as highly significant as it gave rise to the first concerted challenge to the 'classic' post-war welfare state. Under the premierships of both Margaret Thatcher (1979–90) and John Major (1990–97), the welfare state was subjected to critical scrutiny and attack. Where once the welfare state had been regarded as an efficiently run institution staffed by dedicated professionals providing security for all on the basis of common citizenship, it was now being portrayed as costly, ineffective and provider dominated. Instead of being seen as an essential pillar of post-war British society, the welfare state was now being blamed for contributing to economic failure and for causing a deeper social malaise. Too many citizens, it was argued, wanted to exercise their rights to welfare without accepting their responsibilities to secure paid employment and support their families.

The growing influence of neo-liberal ideas within the Conservative party following successive election defeats in 1974 will be discussed in the first section of this chapter. Attention will then turn to the record of the Thatcher governments between 1979 and 1990. Did they make a concerted attempt to *dismantle* the welfare state or did they merely pursue a 'neo-liberal' *reform* strategy? The welfare record of the Major governments from 1990 to 1997 will be discussed in the third section of the chapter. Did Major continue the Thatcher 'revolution' or did he change direction? Finally, the question of whether the Thatcher and Major governments represented a departure from traditional conservatism will be considered.

Neo-liberal ascendancy within the Conservative party: the forward march of Thatcherism

Edward Heath's consecutive defeats in the General Elections of February and October 1974 served to galvanize 'liberal' opinion, which Enoch Powell most notably, had endeavoured to keep alive (Shepherd 1996) within the Conservative Party. The maintenance of traditional Conservative values, such as 'sound' money, social order and limited state intervention, was now judged to require a more 'confrontational' form of economic and social policy. It was believed that a retreat from corporatism and interventionism was essential if the nation was to return to economic prosperity and social stability (Gamble 1988).

One of the key protagonists in this debate was Keith Joseph, who had been a high spending Minister at the Department of Health and Social Security in the previous Heath government (1970–74). Converted to the merits of monetarism by influential neo-liberals such as Alfred Sherman, Peter Bauer, Ralph Harris and Alan Walters, Joseph was now persuaded that the pursuit of 'true' Conservatism required the wholesale rejection of the interventionist approach that both Labour and Conservative governments had pursued since the Second World War. In a series of well-publicized speeches, Joseph argued that combating inflation, rather than unemployment, was the principal task for a modern government (Cockett 1995). He also alerted his audiences to the negative impact of the post-war state welfare state. Previously, he had doubted that there was any causal relationship between state welfare support and a so-called dependency culture (Joseph 1959). Now he was convinced that 'a generous welfare system could produce a harmful form of dependency after all' (Denham and Garnett 2001: 101).

The Centre for Policy Studies, which Heath permitted Joseph to establish in May 1974 (even though it might undermine the work of the Party's own Research Department under its then director Chris Patten), became an important institutional base for Joseph's revisionism. Although its explicit rationale was to explore aspects of the European social market model which might be adopted in Britain, the Centre 'quickly became the crucible of Joseph's intellectual revolution – a meeting place where those interested in changing the party's thinking could meet to discuss their ideas before separating to write papers and pamphlets' (Campbell 2000: 266). Joseph became chair of this new organization, Margaret Thatcher was appointed as vice chair and Alfred Sherman became the Centre's Director.

Carefully crafted by Sherman, Joseph's speeches attracted considerable publicity. In a speech in Birmingham (that was republished in full in *The Times* shortly after the Conservative's second electoral defeat in October 1974), Joseph criticized the welfare state for creating a dependency culture. His comments on the need to prevent the growth of single motherhood within working-class communities proved highly controversial. According to Joseph, these mothers were undermining the 'human stock' of the nation by 'producing problem children', who would become delinquent and end up in borstals, 'abnormal educational establishments' and prisons (quoted in Raison 1990: 91). The eugenic undertones of these remarks provoked a sharp response from Joseph's opponents (Charmley 1996: 197–8). Adverse criticism, as well as personal doubts about his suitability to lead the Conservative Party, persuaded Joseph not to stand as the neo-liberal candidate (Harrison 2004) when Heath finally indicated that there would be a post-election leadership contest (Campbell 1993).

With Edward Du Cann following Joseph's lead, there appeared to be no senior figure in the Party willing to stand against Heath on a 'neo-liberal' platform. The void was filled by Margaret Thatcher. Following an astute campaign, masterminded by Airey Neave, Thatcher obtained the support of 130 Conservative MPs compared with 119 for Heath in the first leadership election of January 1975. Although the margin of her first round victory was insufficient to secure the leadership, Thatcher easily defeated four new challengers – Whitelaw, Howe, Prior and Peyton – in the second ballot to become the new Conservative leader (Campbell 1993).

As Leader of the Opposition, Thatcher endured a baptism of fire. She had to overcome sceptics in her own Party who believed that she was little more than a 'narrow minded dogmatist' with 'simple minded remedies' (Campbell 2003: 2) and she also had to pit herself, usually unsuccessfully, against Callaghan during Prime Minister's Question Time (Morgan 1992). It was not until the autumn of 1976 that the Conservatives finally enjoyed a year long period of ascendancy in the opinion polls. However, following the formation of a Lib-Lab pact in March 1977, Labour began to recover ground pulling ahead of their main rivals by the autumn of 1978. As Campbell (2000) points out, just six months prior to becoming Prime Minister, Thatcher was still being written off by many of her critics as 'too suburban, strident, right-wing and inexperienced' to enter Downing Street (p. 319). Fortified by Callaghan's reluctance to call a snap election in the autumn of 1978 and the negative public response to industrial unrest during the so-called 'Winter of Discontent' (see Jefferys 2002: chapter 8), Thatcher emerged victorious in the May 1979 General Election securing a 43-seat overall majority with 43.9% of the popular vote (339 seats) compared with Labour's 36.9% share (269 seats).

The Thatcher governments 1979–90

Neo-liberal influences were clearly visible in the Conservative Party's General Election manifesto of 1979. In her foreword to the manifesto, Thatcher reiterated her belief that enhancing the power of the individual rather than of the state was the key to 'the recovery of our country' (Conservative

Party 1979: 5). The manifesto promised to bring inflation under control through 'proper monetary discipline', to reduce state spending as a proportion of national income by abolishing 'expensive socialist programmes' (p. 9), and to tackle waste and unnecessary bureaucracy. Curbs on picketing and the 'closed shop' (under which union membership was a condition of employment), as well as the 'wider use of secret ballots' were proposed in order to restrain 'trade union power and privileges' (pp. 10–11). Income tax was to be cut 'at all levels to reward hard work, responsibility and success'. Nationalization was firmly rejected in favour of increased private ownership and import controls were ruled out. The fight against crime was to be prioritized and 'firm immigration control for the future' was promised (p. 20). Home ownership was to be encouraged by granting 'council and new town tenants the legal right to buy their homes'. The privately rented sector was to be revitalized. Higher standards were promised in education and the direct grant principle, whereby 'bright children from modest backgrounds' were provided with an opportunity to study at independent schools on a subsidized basis, was to be restored through a new assisted places scheme. NHS spending was to be maintained, but administered more effectively, while 'Labour's vendetta against the private health sector' was to be ended by restoring tax relief for 'employer–employee medical insurance schemes and by allowing pay beds 'where there is a demand for them' (p. 26). In the case of social security, the manifesto promised 'to simplify the system, restore the incentive to work, reduce the poverty trap and bring more effective help to those in greatest need' (p. 27). Unemployment and short-term sickness benefits were to be made liable to tax, while Child Benefit (seen as a key element in the Party's tax credit plans for the future) was to be retained as was the special addition for lone parent families.

Upon their return to office, however, the Conservatives decided not to embark on major structural reform of the welfare state. Although Thatcher, Howe and Joseph were committed ideologically to rolling back the welfare state, they believed that incremental change was preferable to 'revolutionary' change. This approach reflected the fact that neo-liberal thinking on welfare had not as yet given rise to practical policy options. As Timmins (2001) notes, 'It was one thing for the Institute of Economic Affairs (IEA) to say student loans or health vouchers were needed, quite another to devise them' (p. 359). In addition, many of the ministers appointed to Thatcher's first Cabinet in 1979, such as Ian Gilmour, Francis Pym, James Prior and Peter Walker were yet to be persuaded that root and branch welfare reform was required. Indeed, it was not until preferment was given to 'true believers', such as Cecil Parkinson, Norman Tebbit and Nigel Lawson that the prospect of significant reform in the longer term became a possibility.

Even if the Conservatives had been more strongly committed to welfare reform in 1979, they would, in all likelihood, have been unable to pursue this strategy in the face of more pressing matters, such as the control of inflation, the restoration of economic incentives, curbs on the power of trade unions and public expenditure restraint.

First-term economic and social imperatives

Thatcher's new Chancellor, Geoffrey Howe, wasted little time in setting a new economic course for the nation. In his first budget, Howe attempted to cut inflation by introducing money supply targets, by increasing interest rates and by reducing the Public Sector Borrowing Requirement. By the time of his second budget in March 1980, Howe had devised a medium term financial strategy under which fiscal and monetary adjustments would be triggered if indicative targets for the money supply and government borrowing were not reached. Cuts in direct taxation were introduced to boost entrepreneurialism. The standard rate of income tax was reduced from 33 to 30% and the top rate from 83 to 60%. The shift to indirect taxation (VAT was increased from 8 to 15%) was designed to restrain consumption, albeit in a regressive way given that such taxes impact more sharply on the poor.

The fight against inflation, which had soared to 18% in 1980, was not helped by the government's decision to increase both police and army pay in accordance with a manifesto commitment, and to implement the recommendations of the Clegg Commission for sizeable increases in public sector pay. The consequent rise in interest rates led to a slowdown in economic activity as many companies found it difficult to remain competitive particularly in export markets. Output fell sharply and by the autumn of 1981 unemployment stood at 2.8 million, double the level of May 1979. Despite calls from some Cabinet members and, most famously, from 364 economists in a letter to *The Times* in March 1981 (see Howe 2006) for the government to abandon their 'monetarist' experiment, Thatcher was unwilling to contemplate any repeat of the economic U-turn that the Heath government pursued in the early 1970s. This resistance proved 'effective'. Inflation fell to 4.5% by 1983 and productivity increased. However, the price in terms of unemployment (which was in excess of three million in 1982) and manufacturing capacity was severe. As Glynn (1999) notes, 'Tight fiscal and monetary policies coincided with the emergence of sterling as a petro-currency. The result was massive job losses and the elimination of approximately 20 per cent of national manufacturing capacity in the space of one or two years' (p. 189).

The first measures introduced to constrain the power of the trade unions were not as dramatic as some had anticipated. Indeed, according to Morgan (1992), 'Prior's Trade Union Act of 1980 was a moderate measure intended to forestall further attacks on union power' (p. 449). Under this legislation, greater restrictions were placed on official picketing, secondary action by those not directly involved in a dispute was made illegal and closed shop arrangements were subject to tighter controls. However, these measures proved to be only the first stage of union reform. A new Employment Act introduced by Norman Tebbit (who had replaced Prior in 1981) restricted legitimate strike activity still further and allowed for compensation to be paid to those workers dismissed for refusing to join a trade union (Evans 2004). As Clarke (1996) concludes:

> Incremental legislation over the next few years went on to require membership ballots, not only in the regular election of union officials and in sanctioning the existence of political funds, but also before any strike action. This highly effective Fabian process avoided Heath's error of trying to do everything at once, while ultimately tying down the trade unions with a thousand silken cords.
>
> (p. 369)

The Thatcher government's emphasis on economic matters did not mean that social policy issues were ignored. Indeed, the concerted attack on public spending (which the Government's first White Paper on public expenditure had declared to be at 'the heart of Britain's economic difficulties' (Cmnd. 7746 1979), proved to be the biggest threat to the welfare state during the period of the first Thatcher government (Hills 1993). Initial increases in a number of social security benefit payments in fulfilment of an election pledge soon gave way, for example, to a series of cost-cutting measures. These included the abolition of the earnings related elements of unemployment and sickness benefits, as well as reductions in the benefit entitlements of those on strike, switching some of the costs of the sick pay scheme to employers and breaking the earnings link for pensioners and other long-term claimants (Evans 1998). In the sphere of education, expenditure reductions were achieved by means of the 1980 Education Act, which limited the obligations of local authorities to provide schoolchildren with milk, meals and transport. Cuts to the tune of 13% over 3 years were also imposed on the university sector. In accordance with their 1979 manifesto commitment, the NHS was exempted from the Conservatives' cost-cutting exercise but little was done to redress the historic under-funding of the service (Webster 2002). There was a sizeable reduction, however, in the level of public spending on housing and Housing Benefit, which fell by 30% in real terms from 1979/80 to 1982/83 (see Hills 1998).

Although relatively few structural welfare reforms were undertaken by the first Thatcher government, those that were enacted demonstrated a clear desire to pursue a neo-liberal social policy agenda. The decision to press ahead with the sale of council housing, for example, was underpinned by a strong desire to counter the post-war collectivist advance. Although initially uncertain about this policy in the early 1970s, Thatcher soon 'grasped its potential for identifying and rewarding precisely those people whom she wanted to wean from socialism' (Campbell 2003: 233). Under the 1980 Housing Act, council house tenants of at least three years' standing were accorded the right to buy their homes at a discounted price, which varied according to their length of tenure. By 1983, some 500,000 tenants had bought their own homes. As Timmins (2001) notes 'It was to prove, though no one could know it then, the biggest single privatization of the Thatcher era, raising £28 billion over thirteen years – more than the sale of gas, electricity and British Telecom put together' (p. 378). The introduction of the assisted places scheme at a time when education spending was being squeezed coupled with the decision to abolish the Health Services Board, which the previous Labour government had established to phase out NHS pay beds and regulate private hospitals, also reflected the government's desire to follow a neo-liberal direction in social policy.

There were other indicators of the ascendancy of a neo-liberal approach to social policy. A departmental working party was set up in 1981 by Thatcher's first Minister of Health, Patrick Jenkin, to explore alternative funding mechanisms for the NHS. Although this study was halted by his successor Norman Fowler (who recognized the potential political fallout that would arise from moving away from a tax financed service), the possibility of 'reform' was not ruled out. Keith Joseph, who succeeded Mark Carlisle at Education in 1981, considered the possibility of introducing education vouchers (which would allow parents to 'purchase' appropriate schooling for their child), a policy that had long been advocated by the IEA and by prominent right-wing MPs such as Rhodes Boyson (1978). However, the failure of Joseph and his advisers (Stuart Sexton and Oliver Letwin) to come up with effective solutions to counter the long list of practical objections raised by departmental officials, led to a tactical retreat.

Neo-liberal influence can also be detected in a report prepared for Cabinet discussion by the Central Policy Review Staff in the autumn of 1982, which outlined some of the measures that could be employed to constrain projected increases in public spending. These included ending the commitment to increase social security benefits in line with prices, the introduction of private health insurance and withdrawing state funding for higher education. Although there was high level Cabinet opposition to many of these proposals (see Lawson 1992) and subsequent official pronouncements to counter a media outcry (including one from the Prime Minister declaring that 'the National Health service is safe with us'), few were left in any doubt about the direction the neo-liberals would take if conditions proved favourable (Young 1993).

Public unease about Conservative plans for the welfare state, high levels of unemployment and the serious disturbances in Brixton, Toxteth and Moss Side might, at other points in history, have contributed to a government defeat at the 1983 General Election. As it transpired, the Conservatives, buoyed up by a recovery in the world economy, a successful military campaign in the Falklands in 1982 (see Green 2006: chapter 6) and a divided opposition (disillusioned former ministers Roy Jenkins, David

Owen, Shirley Williams and Bill Rodgers left the Labour Party to form the Social Democratic Party in 1981; see Crewe and King 1997), managed to increase their overall majority in the House of Commons to 144 seats albeit with a slightly reduced share of the vote (42.4%).

Thatcherism 1983–90

In their General Election manifesto of 1983, the Party had highlighted their achievements in cutting taxes, controlling public expenditure, creating an enterprise economy, protecting pensioners 'against rising prices' and strengthening the NHS (*The Conservative Manifesto 1983*, reproduced in Dale 2000a: 287). In their second term they proposed to introduce further trade union reforms, create more flexible labour markets, press ahead with privatization, widen share ownership and council house sales, promote private health insurance, increase parental choice in education, maintain effective immigration controls and abolish the metropolitan councils and the Greater London Council. It was hoped that developments of this kind would appeal not only to the Party faithful, but also to those aspiring skilled workers who were becoming attracted to the 'Thatcherite' cause (Dorey 1995).

The second term 1983–87

During the second term of the Thatcher government (1983–87) economic reform remained the central focus. This was never better illustrated than by the government's response to the national coal strike of 1984–85, which they were determined to break in order to weaken trade union power and pave the way for the future privatization of the industry. By adhering closely to the so-called 'Ridley formula', which decreed that the miners could only be defeated by the 'build-up of coal stocks and imports, the encouragement of non-union road hauliers to move coal, the rapid introduction of dual coal-oil firing at all power stations, the withdrawal of social security benefits from strikers' families and the creation of a large, mobile squad of police' (Milne 2004: 9), the government emerged 'victorious' albeit after a bitter year-long dispute.

The government also accelerated its privatization programme, which it believed would bring efficiency gains, as well as a valuable income stream for the Treasury. Various concerns such as Cable and Wireless, Associated British Ports, British Aerospace, Britoil and Amersham International had been transferred either in whole or part to the private sector during the first Thatcher administration. More wide-ranging sales were now undertaken. British Telecom was sold for £4 billion in 1984, while some £5.4 billion was realized by the sale of British Gas in 1986. Crucially, these sales proved popular with traditional Labour supporters. As Morgan (1992) observes, privatization was 'a huge success in socio-political terms, in vastly expanding the range of the shareholding classes. It made privatization part of a wider cultural shift among the British people, including wide swathes of the working class. Many hundreds of thousands of trade unionists were among those who became shareholders for the first time' (p. 469).

Greater central control was also exercised over local government spending through the introduction of 'rate capping', which restricted the rights of councils to increase rate charges above Treasury guidelines. The manifesto pledge to abolish both the Greater London Council and the six metropolitan councils and to devolve their powers to the London boroughs and metropolitan districts was also carried through, despite spirited resistance (Evans 2004).

Second term social policy

There was, however, no major onslaught on the welfare state along neo-liberal lines during the second term. As Glennerster (2007) notes, 'At the end of two terms in office, despite her dramatic confrontations with the Argentinians and the miners, large-scale privatization and trade union reform, Mrs Thatcher had still to tackle social policy in a radical way' (p. 190). Nicholas Ridley (1991), a government minister of the period, shares this assessment, contending that the Prime Minister 'ought to have put in place alternative methods of provision based on the private sector which gave the people both choice and the quality of service they wanted. Her steps in this direction were too late, too hesitant, and not radical enough' (p. 257).

The lack of substantive structural welfare reform in the second term did not, however, signify any let up in the 'ideological' attack on the welfare state. State welfare provision continued to be portrayed as both inefficient and ineffective. The public was being softened up for the major reforms that were to be brought forward during Thatcher's third term.

Further tax cuts and curbs on public spending remained key concerns for Thatcher and her new Chancellor, Nigel Lawson, who, like his predecessor Geoffrey Howe, was keen to secure cuts in welfare spending.

Social security

Given its relatively large budget, social security was one area targeted for budget reductions. While the Minister for Health and Social Security – Norman Fowler – was quite prepared to cut 'unnecessary spending', such as the universal death grant, he believed it was his responsibility 'to prevent unnecessary cuts' (Fowler 1991: 206–7). Accordingly, he embarked on a review of some key areas of social security in order to ensure that future spending was targeted on those in greatest need.

This in-depth, transparent, cost-neutral review focused on four aspects of the social security system – pensions, housing benefit, supplementary benefits, and benefits for children and young people (see Deakin 1994). In the subsequent Green Paper (Cmnd. 9517 1985) various recommendations were put forwards including the abolition of the State earnings-related pension scheme (SERPS), the renaming of Supplementary Benefit (SB) as Income Support, the introduction of a Social Fund (based mainly on loans, rather than grants) to replace various discretionary SB payments, a new Family Credit scheme (to supersede Family Income Supplement) and a streamlined Housing Benefit scheme. According to Timmins (2001), 'families with children and the elderly' stood to gain 'marginally from the changes at the expense of the unemployed, those without children and particularly those under twenty-five whose benefit was cut markedly in an attempt to cajole them to either stay in the parental home or get into work' (p. 399). As it transpired, a number of these proposals were modified before the eventual passage of the 1986 Social Security Act. The most significant of these related to SERPS. Treasury concerns that the abolition of SERPS would prove costly in the short term, coupled with doubts about the viability of alternative private arrangements, led to a compromise decision to retain a much less generous version of the state scheme that would still deliver substantial savings to the public purse in the longer term.

Although this review did not generate any short-term savings for the Treasury it did, in the words of Chancellor Lawson (1992), stem 'the escalation that would otherwise have occurred' (p. 593). Importantly, this review also demonstrated the practical difficulties involved in dismantling the welfare state. The Fowler Review did, however, confirm that it was possible to press ahead with incremental change both in terms of the scope of welfare services and their administration.

The National Health Service

Of course opting for reform rather than revolution brought its own set of difficulties. In the case of the NHS, the reforms needed to be designed in such a way that they would not leave the government open to the charge that they were intent on dismantling the NHS. Equally, though, tentative reforms would do little to bring health spending under control. The solution to this quandary was an attempt to improve the performance of the NHS by making better use of existing resources.

Five significant efficiency measures were introduced during Thatcher's second term (Ham 1999). First, health authorities were required to review their existing budgets and generate annual efficiency savings. Secondly, so-called Rayner scrutinies (named after the retailer Derek Rayner, who had been seconded as a government advisor in 1979) were introduced in an effort to secure major economies in areas such as transport services, advertising and staff accommodation. Thirdly, performance indicators were introduced in 1983 so that the functioning of one health authority could be compared with others in terms of length of hospital stay, treatment costs and waiting lists. Fourthly, in an effort to see whether costs could be reduced in some non-medical services, such as cleaning, catering and laundry services, potential providers were invited to tender for these services. Although many of these contracts were awarded to in-house teams (around 90%), rather than private competitors, a downward pressure on costs was achieved by reducing the incomes of already poorly paid workers. It is estimated that this tendering process generated around £110 million worth of 'savings' during its first year in operation. Fifthly, the government secured further cost savings by limiting the number of 'branded' drugs that GPs could prescribe to NHS patients. As Klein (1995) notes, the limited list system challenged 'the idea that clinical autonomy bestowed an automatic, unfettered right to use public resources without scrutiny or limits' (p. 165).

The introduction of management structures that mirrored those operating in the private sector were deemed essential in order to prevent provider 'interests' derailing the drive for efficiency. Roy Griffiths, the managing director of the supermarket chain Sainsbury's, was commissioned to conduct an inquiry into NHS management in 1983. In a succinct report, Griffiths recommended the replacement of 'unfocussed consensual styled administrative practices by a more clearly defined management structure' (see Klein 1995). Although the implementation of this new public management model proved problematic, opposition to these changes was muted, not least because of a government victory over the trade unions in a pay dispute involving nurses and ancillary staff in 1982 (see Fowler 1991: chapter 9). As a result, a commercial style managerial ethos quickly became embedded within the NHS and was soon extended to other parts of the public sector (Pollitt 1993).

One of the supposed virtues of this 'new' public management was that it would help welfare providers to focus more sharply on the needs of service users. The government was keen to ensure that providers regarded service users more like consumers who could take their custom elsewhere if provision proved unsatisfactory. The government's desire to prioritize the interests of welfare consumers, rather than providers, led to the deregulation of optical services in 1984 (Fowler 1991). This was followed by the publication of a Green Paper on primary health care in 1986 (Cmnd. 9771 1986), which aimed to 'stimulate competition for patients among GPs, getting them to enter something more like a market in which patients would have more choice and GPs would have to be more responsive' (Timmins 2001: 413).

Education

Given Keith Joseph's lengthy tenure as Secretary of State for education (1981–6), major reforms might have been anticipated in this area of social policy. Certainly, Joseph was keen to restrain spending, improve the attainment levels of poorly performing pupils, challenge provider interests and engender more positive approaches to enterprise within schools and universities. Although he prepared the ground for future reforms, he found it difficult to bring about fundamental change during his period of office. This failure was not for want of trying. Joseph remained keen, for example, to introduce education vouchers. As Timmins (2001) notes:

> The idea was beguilingly simple. Parents would get a voucher with which to 'buy' education at the school of their choice. Schools, forced to compete, would become more responsive. Good schools would expand, bad ones would improve or close. Parents – not teachers, the edu-cational establishment or local and national politicians – would thus determine the nature of schools and would more than likely reopen the door to selection. Education would become consumer – not producer – run and local authority control of it would be broken.
>
> (p. 418)

However, it proved immensely difficult to devise a workable voucher scheme. By the time of the 1983 Conservative Party Conference Joseph was forced to announce that, despite his personal commitment to vouchers, there was no imminent prospect of such a scheme being introduced.

Joseph's commitment to expenditure restraint landed him in hot water. In 1984, his plan to secure savings of £39 million by requiring higher income parents to contribute towards the tuition fees of their children studying at university was speedily withdrawn in the face of vociferous parental and backbench opposition (Harrison 2004). Moreover, his unwillingness to offer teachers a generous pay award led to a lengthy period of industrial action from February 1985 to May 1986. The dispute was eventually resolved by his successor, Kenneth Baker, who, having secured £2.4 billion in additional funding from the Chancellor, was able to offer teachers a more attractive remuneration package (Timmins 2001).

Joseph did make progress in other areas. Greater scrutiny of school per-formance was facilitated by the publication of Her Majesty's Inspectorate (HMI) reports and by requiring schools to provide an annual report for parents. Reforms in the provision for non-academically inclined pupils were implemented by giving the Department of Employment and the Manpower Services Commission greater control over technical and vocational education. Joseph's Green Paper on higher education (Cmnd. 9524 1985) encouraged universities to consider how they could better respond to the nation's economic priorities. Joseph's decision to change the name of the Social Science Research Council to the Economic and Social Research Council was symbolic of his entrepreneurial leanings heralding as it did the development of 'utilitarian', rather than scholarly, research agendas.

Housing

Given the success of their first term housing strategy, the Conservatives saw little need for major reform during the second phase of Thatcherism. Consolidation of earlier achievements was seen to be the best way forward. Accordingly, the sale of council housing was further encouraged by the introduction of ever more generous discounts. New house building was concentrated in the private sector, while central government concerns about the competence of local authority landlords ensured that the dwindling amount of new public sector house building (30,000) was undertaken mainly by housing associations (see Malpass 2005). In addition, the pressure on local authorities to increase council house rents to market levels continued as a result of the withdrawal of central government subsidies. By 1986–87, only 25% of local authorities were still receiving such subsidies (Hills 1998: 127).

Towards the end of 1986, Thatcher set up a number of high profile, ministerial-led, policy groups to produce a programme for a third term in government. The ideas emanating from these groups formed the backbone of the Party's General Election manifesto of 1987, which Thatcher (1995) considered the finest the Conservatives had ever produced.

Thatcher's last stand (1987–90)

Although Thatcher's final period in office has come to be regarded as the most significant in terms of the Conservative 'revolution', the 1987 manifesto itself provided little evidence of any real change of direction. The manifesto promised to enhance personal freedom and prosperity by controlling inflation, lowering taxes (when prudent) and ensuring that as many citizens as possible had the opportunity to become home owners or shareholders. The ideological importance of wider share ownership was made explicit. 'Owning a direct stake in industry not only enhances personal independence; it also gives a heightened sense of involvement and pride in British industry. More realistic attitudes to profit and investment take root' (Conservative Party 1987: 16–17). Further trade union reforms were to be introduced and the proportion of national income devoted to public expenditure was to be reduced. A more detailed social policy agenda was set out, but this did not represent a radical departure from the 'gradualist' approach to reform, which had been followed since 1979.

The one social policy area in which significant reforms were proposed was education. Four major school initiatives were set out – the introduction of a National Curriculum, devolved budgetary control for 'all secondary schools and many primary schools' (Conservative Party 1987: 18), increased parental choice and opportunities for schools to opt out of local education authority (LEA) control.

Less dramatic change was proposed in other areas of welfare. Health care was to be improved by a greater emphasis on prevention, the promotion of community care, support for NHS staff, more modern facilities and stronger management. In the sphere of social security, the Conservatives pledged to maintain the value of the state retirement pension and to encourage the 'ten million employees who do not yet have their own occupational scheme to have a pension of their own'. They also pledged to provide additional help for low income families, to 'improve the framework of benefits for disabled people' and to 'reform the tangled web of income-related benefits which has grown up over forty years' (pp. 53–4). Finally, in the case of housing, the Conservatives now sought to increase owner occupation, regenerate the privately rented sector, provide council tenants with a greater choice of landlords and transform the worst housing estates through the creation of Housing Action Trusts, who would be permitted 'to take over such housing, renovate it, and pass it on to different tenures and ownerships' (p. 15).

The Welfare State: a radical reform agenda?

The manifesto only hinted at the more radical restructuring of the welfare state that the Party was to undertake following their third consecutive election victory in June 1987, in which their majority was reduced to 101 seats (with 42% of the vote). This may have reflected a decision to refrain from disclosing their true policy intentions for fear of voter antipathy. Alternatively, there are good grounds for suggesting that the government's decision to press ahead with a more radical policy agenda was linked to post election issues. Certainly, Mrs Thatcher's surprise announcement on the BBC television programme *Panorama* in January 1988 that she was setting up a wide-ranging review of health care fits with this latter explanation (Klein 1995). Since their election victory the government had been subjected to renewed criticism about its stewardship of the National Health Service including a well publicized reprimand from the Presidents of the Royal Colleges in December 1987. Thatcher was determined to tackle such critics head on.

Health and community care reforms

The small NHS review team that Thatcher established consisted of just five ministers (the Prime Minister, John Moore, Tony Newton, Nigel Lawson and John Major), three deputy secretaries and a number of policy unit advisors. Radical changes to the NHS such as greater reliance on the private sector or increased charges were ruled out on economic and political grounds. Indeed, the Chancellor was persuaded that one of the key advantages of retaining the NHS was that it provided opportunities for cost containment which few other systems could rival (Lawson 1992). Accordingly, the review focused on reforming the NHS along the lines suggested by the influential health expert Alain Enthoven (1985). This involved the creation of an internal market with a division between purchasers and providers of health services that would increase efficiency and contain costs. The review team found it difficult, however, to devise a practical way forward and it was not until Kenneth Clarke joined the team (having replaced John Moore at Health in July 1989) that significant progress was made (Timmins 2001). It was eventually agreed that District Health Authorities should become purchasers of care and that hospitals should be transformed into self-governing trusts free from the constraints of health authority control. A GP fund holding scheme under which doctors would be provided with a budget to purchase services for their patients from a range of providers was also to be introduced. It was envisaged that this scheme would pave the way for a patient-led health service.

These proposals formed the cornerstone of the White Paper *Working for Patients* (Cm. 555 1988) and the National Health Service and Community Care Act of 1990. Although these reforms were vigorously opposed both by the Labour Party and the BMA, whose memorable advertising campaign included the use of a steamroller to depict 'Mrs Thatcher's plans for the NHS'. Clarke, displaying a 'Bevanite' resolve, was able to implement his radical reforms with few concessions (Timmins 2001; Glennerster 2007).

The reform of community care highlighted the quasi neo-liberal approach to welfare reform that the Conservatives now favoured. Instead of outright abolition or privatization, the welfare state was to be transformed from within. Reviews of community care, such as the Audit Commission Report of 1986, had highlighted problems with the quality of such provision, its organization and its cost. The latter was of particular concern. Indeed, social security spending on residential care rose from £10 million in 1981 to over £2 billion by 1991 as relatives, local authorities and care providers lay claim to this funding source. Roy Griffiths (1988) was asked to come up with a solution. His recommendations which included the appointment of a Minister of Social Care, the ring fencing of resources and a lead role for local authorities were not greeted with any initial enthusiasm by either Thatcher or Clarke who were uneasy about the extent of local authority involvement

(Timmins 2001). However, once it became clear that it would be possible to restrict the role of local authorities to one of co-ordination, rather than provision, a politically acceptable reform programme emerged. The reforms, which were finally implemented in 1993, led to budgetary responsibility for community care being given to local councils rather than the Department of Social Security. Importantly, though, local authorities were to have an enabling rather than a provider role (Ridley 1991). Their key responsibilities were to prepare a community care plan, conduct need assessments, arrange inspections of residential homes and fund service providers. Although local authorities could act as residual 'arms length' providers, their main task was to contract out care provision to the private and voluntary sectors thereby encouraging competition, innovation and economy. As Glennerster (2007) concludes, 'the reform of community care thus fitted into what was now emerging as the common pattern of social policy reforms in the Thatcher period – continued state funding but a variety of private and public providers' (p. 208).

Education, social security and housing reforms

Despite concerted opposition from education professionals and the Labour Party, the Conservatives pushed ahead with their third-term education reforms. Under the 1988 Education Reform Act, a ten-subject National Curriculum was introduced for all state schools, as well as requisite attainment levels (knowledge, skills and understanding) that pupils would be expected to demonstrate through national testing at the ages of 7, 11, 14 and 16. The results of such tests were to be publicized in order to give parents greater information about the standards being achieved by different schools. The Act also paved the way for the introduction of grant maintained (GM) schools, which would be permitted to opt out of local authority control (after a 'parental' ballot) and receive their funds directly from the Department of Education. Non-GM schools were also given greater autonomy under a local management of schools (LMS) initiative, which permitted head teachers and their governing bodies to exercise greater control over expenditure and staff appointments. Parental choice was also enhanced by allowing popular local schools to admit more pupils if there was spare capacity. Privately sponsored (but largely state-funded) City Technology Colleges were also to be established in an effort to create centres of educational excellence in those educationally disadvantaged neighbourhoods where the comprehensive system was deemed to have failed.

There were, in contrast, no major reforms in social security during the early years of the third term. This was to be expected given that many of the Fowler reforms needed time to bed in. Implementation proved to be far from straightforward especially in the case of Housing Benefit where the new

Minister, John Moore, was forced to reverse some of the Fowler cuts after their onerous impact on many low income families became a source of backbench concern. However, Moore's inclination was always to shift social policy in a neo-liberal direction, targeting resources wherever possible on the more 'deserving' (see Lowe 2005: 356). As part of the 1987 spending round, he readily agreed to freeze Child Benefit (a policy he continued in the following year), using some of the resources released for the means-tested Family Credit scheme. He also withdrew the right of 16- and 17-year-olds to claim Income Support once this group had been guaranteed a Youth Training Scheme place. Given his short tenure in office, Moore has attracted limited critical attention. In many ways, he is the forgotten man of 'Thatcherism'. However, as Timmins (2001) reminds us, his 'cultural' legacy should certainly not be overlooked. Influenced by commentators such as Charles Murray (1980), Moore was committed to a smaller state and selective welfare provision. He questioned the way in which left-of-centre researchers and commentators had failed to distinguish between poverty and inequality, and did much to ensure that the term welfare came to be associated with feckless dependency, rather than a positive aspect of citizenship. As Timmins (2001) concludes, 'If language shapes an agenda, Moore played his part' (p. 450).

In housing, the Conservatives recognized that their highly successful council house sales policy could not continue indefinitely as both the stock of available housing and the pool of those who could afford to buy dwindled. However, as the manifesto had made clear, they remained committed to reducing the state's role in the construction, ownership, administration and regulation of housing, and reviving the privately rented sector. Under the 1988 Housing Act, private landlords or housing associations were permitted to take over the running of council housing in a given locality if they could secure the support of existing tenants by means of a ballot. Housing Action Trusts were encouraged, rent controls were abolished and landlords were able to let property on an assured or shorthold basis. Moreover, tenants not eligible for Housing Benefit faced steep rises in rent levels as a result of the withdrawal of central government subsidies and the inability of local authorities to subsidize rents from general revenues.

In practice, these housing reforms were not particularly successful. Only five Housing Action Trusts had been established by 1994 as tenants opted to stay with their local authority landlords. Although some of the council stock passed from local authorities to alternative landlords, this was rarely the result of so-called 'Tenants' Choice'. Transfers were generally instigated by Conservative-controlled local authorities in the south of England who were keen to dispose of their housing stock. By 1994 some 3.7 million homes remained under council control compared with 4.2 million in 1988 (Timmins 2001).

Recognizing that the positive co-operation of civil servants was crucial to the success of their welfare and other reforms, the Conservatives attempted to challenge what they perceived to be a deep-seated preference for collectivism in the corridors of Whitehall. To this end some 60 decentralized, quasi-autonomous 'executive agencies' (QUANGOS) were established under the so-called Next Steps initiative. These new operational agencies were to function in similar ways to commercial organizations. They were headed up by directors recruited predominantly from the private sector on fixed-term contracts with remuneration packages linked to the achievement of agreed performance targets. This 'cultural' transformation was complemented by a decision to ensure that all positions in the 'entire upper echelons of Whitehall' were filled by Thatcher appointees by the end of her second term in office (Campbell 2003: 44).

On reflection, the period from 1987 to 1990 was highly significant in term of the history of the post-1945 welfare state. Although the various elements of the welfare state remained intact to a greater or lesser extent, the Conservatives proved adroit in changing its underlying character and ethos. By challenging commonly held assumptions about the selflessness of state welfare providers and their ability to make effective use of taxpayer funds, as well as by championing service users, the Conservatives succeeded in promoting the idea that the 'good' citizen should approach state welfare provision with the same level of discernment they employed in their role as a customer. If a welfare revolution had occurred, it was in the hearts and minds of the British people, rather than in the structures of the welfare state.

Thatcher's demise

Although Margaret Thatcher's position as leader of the Conservative Party appeared unassailable at the time of the 1987 General Election, a combination of events led to her dramatic downfall less than three years later. The short post-election economic boom had given way to a recession in 1989 and the unpopularity of the Community Charge or Poll Tax (which was seen as imposing unfair burdens on those on low or moderate incomes) gave rise to a highly effective, broad based, anti-poll tax campaign, which culminated in a mass demonstration in Trafalgar Square in March 1990. Thatcher was also weakened by a series of ministerial resignations. Michael Heseltine took his leave in 1986 over the Westland helicopter affair, followed by Leon Brittan. Norman Tebbit left the government to care for his wife (who had been seriously injured in the Brighton bombing of 1984) immediately after the 1987 election victory (see Evans 2004). Nigel Lawson departed in 1989 after becoming increasingly frustrated by Thatcher's desire to follow the advice of her economic guru, Alan Walters, rather than his own on key issues such as joining the Exchange Rate Mechanism. Fowler and Walker opted to leave the Cabinet early in 1990 and Nicholas Ridley (1991) resigned later that summer after some 'Basil Fawlty' style comments about the Germans in *The Spectator*.

> By the autumn of that year Thatcher's position had become fragile. The British economy was experiencing recession, the European Union was moving in a direction at odds with her conception of European unity, there was palpable unease within the Conservative parliamentary party and the cabinet, and all of this was compounded and exacerbated by the troubles generated by the poll tax.
>
> (Green 2006: 8)

The denouement took place in November 1990 when Thatcher's longest serving minister, Geoffrey Howe, left the government after yet another prime ministerial anti-European tirade, famously declaring in his Commons resignation speech that his 'cricket bat' had been broken by his own team captain (Howe 1990). A year earlier, Thatcher had comfortably seen off a leadership challenge from Sir Anthony Meyer. Now she faced a much more dangerous challenger in the shape of Michael Heseltine. Although Thatcher polled 204 votes to Heseltine's 152 the margin of victory proved insufficient (albeit by just four votes) to prevent a second ballot. After consulting Cabinet colleagues (some of whose responses she regarded as 'treacherous') and others such as the maverick Labour MP Frank Field, she resigned from office, acknowledging that her 'friends and allies' now regarded her as an electoral liability rather than an asset (Thatcher 1995: 855).

The Thatcher 'revolution' and the Welfare State

In assessing the significance of the Thatcher footprint on the welfare state, it is important to recognize that her desire to reform this institution formed part of a broader strategy to bring about the realignment of British society. The overarching objective of 'Thatcherism' was to counter the 'malign' influence of outmoded socialist ideas and practice on both economic and social policy (Jenkins 2006). The attack on socialism was deemed to require a significant diminution of trade union influence, the creation of a more self-interested, independent and entrepreneurial citizenry, and radical changes in the welfare state. The ultimate success of this strategy was to be judged by whether a future Labour government would be able to win a General Election on a socialist platform.

The first of these aims, curbing the influence of the trade unions, was achieved by refusing to enter into any corporatist agreements or incomes policies, by the introduction of legislative reforms and by standing up to those trade union leaders, who were deemed to be more concerned with overthrowing the government than pursing the 'real' interests of their members. High levels of unemployment and a sharp decline in manufacturing which led to a fall in trade union membership from 52% of the workforce in 1979 to 37% by 1990 undoubtedly helped the Conservatives in their pursuit of this aim. By the end of her period in office, Thatcher could justly claim to have created a weak and increasingly ineffectual trade union movement.

In pursuit of their second aim, the creation of a more individualist citizenry, the Conservatives introduced a range of measures to persuade citizens to focus on personal and familial well-being, rather than collective concerns. Appeals to 'aspiring' citizens included tax cuts, extended forms of home ownership and guaranteed windfalls from buying shares in privatized public utilities. It is difficult to assess the extent to which the Conservatives succeeded in achieving a cultural transformation in British society. Although many commentators have drawn attention to the emergence of a more individualistic culture (see Black 2004), the evidence from large scale studies, such as the British Social Attitudes survey does not support the case for significant cultural change (see Park *et al.* 2003).

As we have seen in relation to the welfare state, reform rather than revolution proved to be the order of the day. Lowe (2005) contends, for example, that although there was a serious attack on 'the economic foundations of the classic welfare state' during this period there was 'no such dismantling' in the sphere of social policy. 'The management of each major service was radically overhauled; but the cost and scope of the government's responsibilities remained largely unimpaired' (p. 370). For Timmins (2001) a 'remarkable paradox' was evident at the end of the Thatcher era:

> A woman whose instincts were to unscramble the NHS and to increase charges, to roll back social security and social services, and to return schools to selection and fee paying, had instead headed a government which found itself promoting reforms that, however controversial, were plainly intended to improve existing health, education and social services. Each of them through the structures they introduced might make future privatization easier, but none of them automatically produce that result.
>
> (p. 476)

Finally, after a meticulous assessment of the Thatcher record, Glennerster (2007) concludes 'that it was the reformers and not the abolitionists who won' (p. 192).

Why, to the regret of many neo-liberal protagonists, did the Thatcher governments opt for welfare reform, rather than revolution (Green and Lucas 1992; Bell *et al.* 1994)? Various factors played a part. First, despite outwards appearances to the contrary, Thatcher proved to be a cautious politician when it came to welfare reform, especially in areas which remained popular with the public such as the NHS (Lawson 1992; Green 2006). Secondly, the practical difficulties involved in introducing neo-liberal measures such as education vouchers or health insurance coupled with potentially high transitional costs convinced economic liberals, such as Lawson (1992), of the merits of measured reform. The injection of a private sector ethos into the delivery of public services, improved targeting, cost containment measures and the greater 'consumer' choice came to be seen as equally effective tools for bringing about neo-liberal style change as outright abolition. In the same way that Crosland believed that a socialist society could be created without resorting to widespread nationalization, so the 'Thatcherites' came to recognize that the more individualistic, market driven Conservative society they wanted to establish could be achieved by reforming, rather than dismantling, the welfare state.

Forward with Major 1990–97: the 'revolution' consolidated?

Steadying the ship 1990–92

John Major, the favoured candidate of Margaret Thatcher, topped the second ballot for the leadership of the Conservative Party in November 1990. Although his tally of 185 votes was two short of the absolute majority required for victory, he was elected as leader following the decision of his two opponents – Michael Heseltine (131) and Douglas Hurd (56) – to bow out of the contest.

Major's sole short-term objective was to secure a fourth consecutive election victory. Two changes were vital if this objective was to be achieved. First, an alternative to the widely despised Poll Tax had to be found. Major's new environment secretary, Michael Heseltine, was given the task of formulating a politically acceptable replacement. By April 1991, he had found a suitable alternative in the shape of a new eight banded property based tax. As Jenkins (2006) observes, 'never was a British tax invented so fast or accepted with such relief' (p. 173). The fact that this new tax would not come into effect until 1993 meant that the impact of the Poll Tax had to be softened by the injection of a £4.5 billion Treasury subsidy in the run up to the General Election of 1992.

Secondly, there was an urgent need to revive an ailing economy. As Deakin (1994) notes, 'Mrs Thatcher had left office with three of four major economic indicators less favourable than when she came in – inflation, unemployment and the balance of payments deficit had all moved in the wrong direction' (p. 188). Industrial productivity proved the exception. Turning the economic curve proved to be a more difficult task. Although the new Chancellor Norman Lamont presided over falls in inflation and interest rates, unemployment remained high. Crucially, though, the new administration seemed, on the basis of opinion poll evidence, to have convinced the public that it could be trusted to rectify the economic problems that it had inherited, but not created (Gilmour and Garnett 1998: 356).

During his first period of office (1990–92) Major attempted to improve the quality of public services through the introduction of the Citizen's Charter in 1991. Major's determination to drive through change in this sphere was prompted in part by his own experiences of:

> ... time pointlessly lost when appointments were not made or kept. Unacceptably long waiting times. Remote council offices, where, after a long bus journey, there was no one available to see you who really knew about the issue ... Anonymous voices and faces who refused to give you a contact name. Offices where correspondence or calls never seemed to be dealt with by the same person and you had to begin from first base, time after time after time.
>
> (Major 2000: 247)

Under the Citizen's Charter service providers were required to devise performance targets (which would be monitored by independent inspectors) deal with user complaints in a more responsive way and provide redress where appropriate (Willman 1994; Lowe 2005).

The Conservative General Election manifesto of 1992 provided few indications, however, that Major wanted to turn away from the policy agenda of the previous Thatcher governments. There were no new ideas. Instead, the manifesto promised renewed commitment to the pursuit of price stability, public expenditure restraint, prudent tax reductions, balanced budgets, and support for 'market mechanisms and incentives' (Conservative Central Office 1992: 5). Plans for the privatization of British Coal, local authority bus companies and airports were unveiled, deregulation was to continue, and the numbers of home owners and shareholders was to increase. The Citizens Charter (which would now be the personal responsibility of a Minister of Cabinet rank) was to be developed further and public services were to be exposed to greater competition and accountability.

The Party's commitment to the NHS was reaffirmed with promises of increased funding, enhanced patient rights and a greater emphasis on preventative services. In terms of social security, the manifesto committed the Party to making further improvements in provision (especially in the sphere of disability benefits) and to the retention of Child Benefit payments for all families. In housing, the reform process was to be continued by giving council tenants increased rights including an option to take a part-share in their home prior to full ownership under a new 'rents to mortgages' scheme. The need to ensure that 'the most important and wide-ranging reforms since the 1940s' (p. 17) were properly embedded was highlighted in relation to education.

Although some commentators seemed confident that Labour would win the 1992 General Election, it is questionable whether this was ever a realistic proposition. The departure of Thatcher, the reform of the Poll Tax and the quiet assurance exuded by Major himself served to focus media attention back on the shortcomings of the Labour leader Neil Kinnock (Harrop and Scammell 1992) and on the party's spending plans, which were portrayed by the Conservatives as a 'tax bombshell'. Despite Labour protestations about the accuracy of the Conservative's arithmetic, the damage had been done. Fears about Labour's economic rectitude led a significant proportion of the electorate to hold tightly onto the hand of 'nurse', in the shape of Major and the Conservatives, for fear of something 'worse' (Kinnock and Labour; see Gilmour and Garnett 1998). The Conservatives polled 'more votes than any party in British political history – 14,092,891', securing 41.9% of the popular vote, but Major's (2000) success was tempered by the fact that this had 'yielded only a miserly majority of seats [21]' (p. 307).

The Major government 1992–97

The main objective of the new Major government was to consolidate the third term reforms. This proved to be far from straightforward in the face of growing economic difficulties. The Chancellor, Norman Lamont, had to grapple with the fallout from the humiliating decision to withdraw from the Exchange Rate Mechanism on 'Black Wednesday' (16 September 1992), when attempts to protect the value of the pound by means of sharp increases in interest rates and £15 billion worth of reserves, proved futile in the face of concerted pressure from currency speculators (Jefferys 2002). A projected budgetary deficit of £50 billion by 1993 led to concerted attempts by neo-liberals within the government and the wider Party to renew their attacks on the welfare state. For example, the No Turning Back Group, which had been established in 1985 to carry forward the Thatcher legacy, published a pamphlet in 1993 recommending major changes in social security, such as the abolition of SERPS and greater reliance on non-state provision for those who were unemployment or disabled. The Home Secretary, Michael Howard, and the Secretary of State for Wales, John Redwood, made well-publicized speeches drawing attention to the way in which the operation of the social security system was leading to an undesirable growth in single motherhood (Page 1997).

Given the deteriorating state of the public finances, the Chief Secretary to the Treasury and influential Thatcher acolyte, Michael Portillo, seized the moment to announce a fundamental review of welfare spending in February 1993. This review, designed to identify those areas where resources could be targeted more effectively or even where the state might withdraw funding completely, received the wholehearted support of Portillo's close political ally, Peter Lilley, the Minister of Social Security. Accepting the case for expenditure constraint, Lilley introduced a range of measures designed to secure a reduction in projected spending by the turn of the century. SERPS payments were to be reduced. Invalidity and sickness benefits were replaced by a new Incapacity Benefit, which included tighter eligibility criteria.

Entitlement to Unemployment Benefit was reduced from 12 to 6 months and a less generous Housing Benefit scheme was brought into effect. A higher pension age for women was to be phased in from 2010, while anti-fraud measures were intensified. Lilley was keen to develop an 'active', rather than 'passive' social security scheme. To this end, various measures were introduced to encourage claimants to return to paid work including a more generous Family Credit scheme and 'back to work' bonuses. One 'welfare to work' scheme, Jobseekers Allowance, which was introduced in 1996, was particularly significant. Under this scheme, claimants had to demonstrate, by documenting the contacts that they had made with prospective employers, that they were actively seeking work. Those deemed to be making insufficient effort to find work faced the prospect of having their benefit reduced. As with Incapacity Benefit, Jobseekers Allowance helped to reduce the claimant count though at the potential cost of increasing the level of unmet need. It also signified the emergence of a social security system in which conditionality had come to the fore (see Deacon 2002). In future the 'right' to benefit would be dependent on a demonstrable willingness on the part of claimants to return to the labour market as quickly as possible or to undergo training that would increase the possibility of securing employment.

Although the new Chancellor, Kenneth Clarke, who replaced Norman Lamont in 1993, was keen to rein in public expenditure, he did not share the apparent enthusiasm of either Portillo or Lilley for a residual welfare state. Indeed, his successful stewardship of the economy served to undermine the economic, as opposed to ideological, case for further welfare reform. Moreover, the fact that so many ministers were finding it difficult to implement previous social policy reforms also served to weaken the case for a further round of reforms.

Consolidation in practice

Education was one area where consolidation was much to the fore. The decision by the new Education Secretary, John Patten, to press ahead with national testing in English for 14-year-olds in 1993, despite professional concerns about the effectiveness of the pilot scheme, eventually led to a national teachers' boycott of *all* testing. The action was only brought to a halt after a more streamlined system had been introduced by one of the government's trusted 'fire fighters', Sir Ron Dearing, the head of the newly established School Curriculum and Assessment Authority.

The introduction of a new external inspection regime for schools, which Major (2000) considered to be 'a key component in improving public service standards' (p. 262), also proved controversial with teachers' unions. Under the leadership of Chris Woodhead, the Office for Standards in Education (OFSTED) adopted a more 'managerial', user focused approach to inspection that differed markedly from the style and tone of HMI's. After the first round of inspections, Woodhead declared that improved standards were needed in 50% of primary and 40% of secondary schools. The minority of schools deemed to have failed their inspection faced the prospect of 'special measures' or even closure.

Despite the incentive of higher funding and a greater freedom to select pupils, relatively few schools, especially in the primary sector and in Scotland, applied for grant-maintained status. By the time of the 1997 General Election only around 4% of all schools had acquired GM status. The national nursery voucher scheme introduced in 1997 to increase parental choice also failed to take root. As Major (2000) reflects, 'Parents had not become used to the new system, LEAs were hostile even as they exploited it, and the private sector was slow to see the advantages it offered' (Major 2000: 399).

In higher education the implementation of the reform agenda proved more straightforward. The idea that universities could receive public funds while remaining autonomous bastions of free thinking was quietly buried. The new contractual system applied by the University Funding Council encouraged universities to become more businesslike and to use their limited resources more effectively. The distinction between universities and polytechnics, which had become increasingly blurred in practice, was ended in 1993 when the latter were permitted to opt for university status.

The new Health Minister, Virginia Bottomley, had to deal with the 'fall-out' from the introduction of the internal market which had led to public concern about whether 'the core NHS values of equity and priority according to need' (Timmins 2001: 514) could be maintained in an era of GP fund holding and hospital reorganization. Although, additional funding was released to meet the initial costs of the reforms, especially the vastly increased managerial wage bill, this was not sustained. As Timmins (2001) notes, 'NHS growth dropped from a real terms increase of almost 6% in 1992–3 to a tenth of that a year later. Bottomley got it up to 3.78 per cent the following year, but it then slid away to barely 1.5% in 1995–6 and 0.6 per cent in the run up to the 1997 election' (p. 516). In such circumstances, it proved hard to meet the ambitious targets for patient health outlined in the *Health of the Nation* (Cm. 1986 1992).

Bottomley's successor, Stephen Dorrell, attempted to allay both public and professional concerns about the adverse impact of the reforms by publishing a White Paper *The National Heath Service: A Service with Ambitions* (Cm. 3425 1996), which played down market influences within the NHS. According to Webster (2002), this document 'reasserted the government's support for the founding principles of the NHS. Its five points of emphasis were: a well-informed public; a seamless service; evidence-based clinical decision making; a more highly trained workforce; and responsiveness to patients' needs. The internal market reforms were relegated to almost adventitious status in the plan for long term development of the NHS' (p. 206).

There were fewer 'consolidation' problems in the sphere of housing. Demunicipalization continued apace. A further 300,000 council houses were sold off in this period, while some 170,000 tenants acquired a new landlord under the large scale voluntary transfer of council housing, following explicit government support for this scheme (Ginsburg 2005). Housing Associations became firmly established as the largest providers of 'social' housing supplying nearly 168,000 new homes in the period from 1992 to 1996 (compared with just 10,500 in the local authority sector; Malpass 2005). Significantly, the rents levied by Housing Associations and other registered social landlords increased in response to rising construction costs occasioned by the requirement to seek private finance rather than rely on public subsidy. Deregulation also appeared to boost the privately rented sector. By 1996 around 2.1 million households were renting privately compared with 1.7 million in 1988 (Timmins 2001: 522).

Back to basics and back to opposition

At the Conservative Party Conference in October 1993, Major (2000) launched a so-called 'back to basics' campaign, which he saw as attempting to challenge the received wisdom of welfare professionals that had 'become divorced from public sentiment and from reality' in areas such as crime, health, education and social work (p. 387). Although Major was clear that his back to basics campaign was 'not about bashing single mothers or preaching sexual fidelity at private citizens' (p. 555), the media took a different line. Following a concerted media campaign, a junior minister, Tim Yeo, was forced to resign after it was revealed that he had fathered an illegitimate child. Another junior minister, Stephen Milligan, was found dead at his home after a sexual misadventure. Ministers and MPs were accused of being willing to allow innocent businessmen to be imprisoned in order to cover up 'illegal' government actions concerning arms for Iraq (the Matrix Churchill case); of asking parliamentary questions in return for payment (Riddick, Tredinnick, Smith and Hamilton); of accepting undeclared hospitality from a Saudi Arabian arms dealer and business associate (Aitken). In contrast to the early 1990s, the Major government now seemed to be engulfed in sleaze.

Since winning the 1992 General Election Major had to contend with persistent sniping from the Eurosceptic wing of his party. He risked losing a parliamentary vote of confidence in order to secure the necessary support for the Treaty of European Union, which had previously been negotiated at Maastricht (this gave Britain an opt out from joining the single currency and the social chapter). Faced with constant attacks on his leadership, Major voluntarily stood for re-election as Party leader in June 1995. Although

Major secured a comfortable victory over his only rival, John Redwood, most commentators perceived that his administration was no longer functioning effectively. As Lowe (2005) notes, his government 'was deeply split over membership of the European Union, besmirched with "sleaze" and beset by a relentless series of crises from fat cats to mad cows' (p. 329). Faced with a vibrant 'New' Labour leader and a reputation for economic failure following the Black Wednesday debacle, it was no longer a question of whether the Conservatives would lose the next General Election, but simply by what margin.

Major: the consolidating 'revolutionary'

Although John Major proved adept at jettisoning unpopular policies at the beginning of his Premiership in the early 1990s and changing the 'mood music' by extolling the virtues of a classless society which would be at 'ease with itself' (Jones 1997; Garnett 2003), he essentially maintained the economically liberal course set by his predecessor. If anything, it could be argued that he was even more pro-active in this sphere, pressing ahead with the privatization of British Coal and British Rail, 'which Mrs Thatcher had prevented Cecil Parkinson [her then Transport Secretary] from even mentioning at the 1990 Party Conference' (Gilmour and Garnett 1998: 368), and abolishing both the National Economic Development Office (1992) and the Wages Councils (1993).

Although Major (2000) was more sympathetic than Thatcher to the virtues of state welfare provision, he continued with the reform agenda of his predecessor. He believed that private sector methods, such as performance-related pay, competition, audit and inspection could improve the performance of service providers. Equally, he remained strongly committed to his Charters, believing that this would eventually encourage social service users to demand a level of service 'comparable to what they would expect from say, Marks & Spencer' (Kavanagh 1994: 10).

Major's commitment to the Thatcherite 'revolution' was confirmed in the Party's General Election manifesto of 1997 (Conservative Central Office 1997). The virtues of the free market, low taxes, privatization, deregulation, shareholding, restrained public spending, low inflation, trade union reform, and tough law and order measures were emphasized. In terms of social policy, the vision of 'a smaller state doing fewer things and doing them better' (p. 29) remained a paramount goal. An affordable and efficient social security system was promised as was a further round of council houses sales. Higher standards and greater choice in education and real terms increases in NHS spending were to be realized. Unfortunately, from Major's perspective, the British public was no longer willing to place their trust in the Conservatives. In a dramatic turn around, the Conservatives lost 182 seats, achieving just 30.7% of the popular vote. 'New' Labour was swept to power with a

179-seat majority on the largest swing to an opposition party since 1945 (43.2% of the popular vote).

A very Conservative welfare revolution?

It has been argued that the approaches adopted by both the Thatcher and Major governments represent a departure from what might be described as 'traditional' Conservatism. In Chapter Two it was argued that Conservative rapprochement with the welfare state in the aftermath of the Second World War did not signal any fundamental shift in either its values or its thinking. Both before and after the Second World War, the Party remained committed to tradition, the nation, the family, social order, capitalism, property rights, and the need for differential rewards and status. Moreover, the Party had long recognized that the means needed to maintain a 'Conservative' society must change with the times. In certain periods, increased 'collectivism' in the form of economic interventionism and welfare reform was judged necessary for Conservatism to flourish. In other eras, less interventionist was seen as the most appropriate way to sustain a Conservative society (Charmley 1996; Blake 1998).

The key question to consider here is whether the means used by the Thatcher and, to a lesser extent, the Major governments to develop and sustain a 'Conservative society' in the period from 1979 to 1997 represented a departure from what might be regarded as the Party's core beliefs and practices. According to one leading modern Conservative, Ian Gilmour (1992), the pursuit of a dogmatic form of economic liberalism in the 1980s and 1990s led to 'social retreat without economic advance' (p. 337), thereby undermining the Party's pragmatic, 'one nation' roots. In contrast, Green (2006) suggests that the approaches adopted by both the Thatcher and Major governments were compatible with 'the Conservative tradition in general', as well as the 'more particular strand of "One Nation" Conservatism' (Green 2006: 42). The evidence reviewed here lends support to this latter perspective. On balance, neither Thatcher nor Major wished to disassociate themselves from traditional Conservative values. They did, however, believe that the economic and social circumstances of the age required rather different means to maintain a Conservative society those that had been employed in the era of Macmillan or Heath.

In the next chapter, attention will turn to the welfare agenda of the New Labour governments of Tony Blair. Were the Blair governments effectively prevented from pursuing a traditional democratic socialist policy agenda as a result of the changes brought about during the Thatcher and Major years? Or had their long years in opposition led to a new phase of 'revisionism' as Labour came to terms with a new set of economic and social circumstances?

Further reading

The memoirs of Thatcher (1995), Major (2000) and other members of the Conservative governments between 1979 and 1997 such as Fowler (1991), Gilmour (1992) and Lawson (1992) provide fascinating insights into social policy and other developments during this period. Useful overviews of this era of Conservative rule have been provided by Timmins (2001), Lowe (2005) and Glennerster (2007), as well as by Deakin (1994), Blake (1998), Gladstone (1999), Campbell (2000, 2003), Evans (2004) and Green (2006).

Revisiting New Labour and the Welfare State

This chapter will focus on the emergence of New Labour and their approach to the welfare state. Following nearly two decades in the political wilderness, the Labour Party finally returned to power in 1997 under the charismatic leadership of Tony Blair. The re-branding of the Party as 'New' Labour was highly significant, indicating as it did a desire to chart a different course from previous post-1945 Labour governments. The first part of this chapter will examine the distinctive features of the New Labour 'project' with particular reference to its welfare strategy. This will be followed by a review of New Labour's social policy record. The chapter will conclude with an assessment of whether New Labour still represents a 'progressive' force in the area of social welfare or whether its retreat from democratic socialism might herald the development of a 'genuine' welfare consensus with the Conservatives.

The emergence of New Labour

Under the leadership of Neil Kinnock (1983–92) and, subsequently John Smith (1992–94), Labour re-positioned itself in an attempt to persuade the public that the Party should be returned to office for the first time since 1979. This re-orientation involved substantial policy revisions including a retreat from public ownership, a 'rapprochement with industry', a firm commitment to 'fiscal and monetary orthodoxy', the retention of Conservative curbs on trade unionism, a revamped welfare agenda and the abandonment of nuclear unilateralism (Shaw 1996: 184–5). This was complemented by organizational reforms, which gave the Party's parliamentary leadership greater power and control. Trade union influence in setting the Party's policy agenda and in selecting its leaders and parliamentary candidates was consequently weakened. In addition, attempts were made to modernize the Party's image by means of improved communications and the introduction of a red rose in 1986 to replace the Party's 'short-lived red flag insignia' (Wring 2005: 94).

The revisionism of Kinnock and, to a lesser extent Smith, provided the platform for the creation of New Labour. Following Smith's premature death in 1994, the Labour Party elected its first 'non-socialist' leader – Tony Blair (Morgan 2004). Under Blair, a concerted effort was made to maximize the party's electoral appeal to 'conservative (small c) suburban working families, the property price-obsessed, and the "middle England" of IKEA, TV "makeover" shows and Britpop' (Chadwick and Heffernan 2003: 2; see also Gould 1998).

On the economic front, New Labour distanced itself from previous Labour governments by embracing the virtues of the market and by its support for a more circumspect approach to state interventionism and public spending. According to two influential New Labour strategists, Peter Mandelson and Roger Liddle (1996), 'New Labour welcomes the rigour of competitive markets as the most efficient means of anticipating and supplying consumers' wants, offering choice and stimulating innovation. Competition is the only effective force that prevents capitalists opting for a quiet life and managers spending their afternoons on the golf-course' (p. 22). Similarly, Giddens (2000) argued that properly regulated markets not only generate 'far greater prosperity than any rival system' but also have 'beneficial effects that go beyond productive efficiency' such as greater choice and personal responsibility (p. 35). In terms of the role of government, Keynesian style intervention was to be abandoned in favour of a rule-based, business friendly economic framework which would create 'stable conditions for investment, trade, and employment by controlling inflation, government borrowing and public spending' (Driver and Martell 2006: 67).

Although New Labour's decision to chart a new economic course was linked to a desire to persuade the electorate of their competence in this sphere, it seems clear that key figures such as Blair, Brown and Mandelson had been persuaded of the need to respond to broader global change in any event (see Finlayson 2003). In a *New Statesman* article published shortly before the Labour Party conference in 1995, Blair makes clear his view on this issue:

> Globalisation is changing the nature of the nation state as power becomes more diffuse and borders more porous. Technological change is reducing the power and capacity of government to control a domestic economy free from external influence. The role of government in this world of change is to represent a national interest, to create a competitive base of physical infrastructure and human skills. The challenge before our party this year is not to slow down the pace of change and get

off the world, but to educate and retrain for the next technologies, to prepare our country for new global competition, and to make our country a competitive base from which to produce the goods and services people want to buy.

(reprinted in Richards 2004: 121)

In a new era of heightened global competition, deregulated financial markets, and a growing reliance on employment in the service sector, rather than in manufacturing, it was argued that the Party needed to sever any lingering attachment to public ownership, planning and deficit financing.

New Labour's initial interest in the more interventionist stakeholder approach to modern capitalism promoted by writers such as Hutton (1994), proved transitory (see Blair 1996a). There were concerns that the interventionist nature of stakeholding might leave New Labour open to the charge of operating like high spending European social democratic governments. Although New Labour accepted that markets required some modest regulation to ensure that inequalities were not reinforced or privileges entrenched (Mandelson and Liddle 1996: 22), they were keen to limit such intervention in order to maximize the dynamism associated with US style 'Anglo Saxon' capitalism (see Jaenicke 2000; Driver 2004).

Blair's pro-market message was endorsed by the Labour Party at a special conference in April 1995 when Clause 4 (section four) of the Party's constitution, which had 'committed' the Party to the common ownership of the means of production, was replaced by a broader generalized statement of aims (Jones 1996; Garnett 2006).

New Labour's support for the market has also led them to adopt a more relaxed approach to disparities of income and wealth. Accepting that 'substantial personal incentives and rewards are necessary in order to encourage risk-taking and entrepreneurialism' (Mandelson and Liddle 1996: 22), New Labour has sought to avoid the criticism that it would govern in a way that penalized economic success. As one leading New Labour insider, Anthony Adonis (1997), points out, 'while New Labour wants to help the poor as a matter of principle, it refuses to hit the rich as a matter of principle. It is this which separates Old Left from New Left' (p. 23).

New Labour's economic reappraisal had important implications for its welfare strategy. It was seen as necessary to move away from the position taken by former advisors in the 1950s and 1960s, such as Abel-Smith, Titmuss and Townsend, that the aim of social policy was to challenge market imperatives (see Ellison 1994). For New Labour, the task was 'to develop an approach whereby welfare policy supports rather than obstructs the operation of a market system, and contributes to the economic goal of competitiveness in a more open economy' (Taylor-Gooby *et al.* 2004: 574).

A significant landmark in this transition was the publication of the report by the Commission on Social Justice (CSJ) in 1994, which had been established by the previous leader John Smith two years earlier (see commentaries by Page 1995 and Townsend 1995). The CSJ (1994) rejected the approaches to the welfare state adopted by both the New Right ('deregulators') and the democratic socialists ('levellers') characterizing the latter as being wedded to the idea that social justice could best be achieved by providing benefits and redistributing income and wealth rather 'than trying to increase opportunities and compete in world markets' (p. 96). The CSJ favoured what it termed as an 'investors' strategy based on a 'proactive' welfare state that sought to reduce citizens' dependency on state support through increased labour market participation if necessary by means of compulsion.

The pro-active welfare message of the CSJ resonated with New Labour thinking. Indeed, the modernization of the welfare state was to become a cornerstone of the New Labour 'project'. Although the policy prescriptions of the post-war Attlee governments were acknowledged as having helped to ameliorate the 'Five Giants' identified by Beveridge (Blair 1995b), more innovative welfare arrangements were now deemed necessary to respond to changes in the labour market, family formations and the growth of consumerism. Moreover, it was argued that the design faults in the 'classic' welfare state, such as 'dependency, moral hazard, bureaucracy, interest-group formation and fraud' needed to be remedied (Giddens 2000: 33).

The political positioning of New Labour

In his foreword to the Labour Party's General Election manifesto of 1997, Tony Blair declared that 'We will be a radical government. But the definition of radicalism will not be that of doctrine whether of left or right, but of achievement. New Labour is a party of ideas and ideals but not of outdated ideology. What counts is what works' (Labour Party 1997: 4). This attempt to portray itself as a 'non-ideological' party pursuing policies best suited to prevailing economic and social circumstances, rather than pursuing a rigid, pre-determined agenda makes it difficult to 'position' New Labour on the political landscape (see Finlayson 2003; Leggett 2004). Not surprisingly, perhaps, 'extrinsic' commentators have offered contrasting views about New Labour's positioning and influences. Huntington and Bale (2002) suggest that New Labour has much in common with Christian democracy; some detect Australian 'Labor' influences (Johnson and Tonkiss 2002; Pierson and Castles 2002), while others highlight the impact of the US Democrats 'new progressivism' (King and Wickham-Jones 1999; Deacon 2000; Driver 2004).

A number of commentators have suggested that New Labour's acceptance of globalization and its embrace of the market have led them to continue with a neo-liberal policy agenda that differs little from the one pursued by the Thatcher and Major governments (Hall 1998, 2003; Hay 1999;

Heffernan 2000). Indeed, the former Conservative Chancellor, Geoffrey Howe (2006) recollects that he used to be 'terrified that Labour spokesmen might mean what they are saying'. Now, following New Labour's conversion to 'Thatcherism', his only concern is 'that they might *not* mean what they are saying' (p. 110). According to Hall (1998), 'the Blair project, in its overall analysis and key assumptions, is still essentially framed by and moving on terrain defined by Thatcherism. Mrs Thatcher had a project. Blair's historic project is adjusting Us to It' (p. 14). Levitas (2005) contends that New Labour has turned away from the redistributionist discourse (RED) of traditional social democracy, which prioritized the reduction of poverty and inequality towards both a social integrationist discourse (SID) and a moral underclass discourse (MUD). SID stresses the importance of paid work, while MUD 'centres on the moral and behavioural delinquency of the excluded themselves' (p. 7).

In contrast, a number of contemporary revisionists reject the suggestion that New Labour has abandoned its commitment to democratic socialism or social democracy (see Fielding 2003a; Rubinstein 1997, 2000; Marquand 2000). According to the former Party leader Neil Kinnock (2000), 'the Labour Party has always embraced innovation, change and newness' (p. 28), while Fielding (2003a) reminds us that 'all successful parties have evolved as circumstances dictated and amended certain of their assumptions to allow them to operate successfully in the new environment. As a result, Labour's past is one of unremitting transformation and adaptation: its history only appears static in retrospect' (p. 217). These revisionists believe that New Labour has remained true to the Party's historic goal of creating a fairer society, but recognize that the means adopted to achieve such an outcome must change in the light of broader economic and social developments. The ends remain 'permanent', the means 'contextual' (Plant 2004: 106).

Certainly, New Labour insiders have insisted that their distancing from many of the policy prescriptions associated with previous Labour administrations, such as nationalization and 'imprudent' levels of public expenditure, should not be equated with a lack of progressive intent. As Brivati (1997) notes, New Labour has been seeking 'a new political foundation which is neither an old style collectivist one nor a new version of neo-liberalism', but rather 'a third position, equidistant from the other two' (p. 184).

The 'third way' and modernized social democracy

New Labour's adoption of a 'third way' position owes much to the work of the sociologist Anthony Giddens (1994), who has questioned the relevance of the left/right distinction in an era that has seen the demise of communism, the growth of global markets, changing family and work patterns, and ever more diverse forms of personal and cultural identity (though see Wetherly 2001). By promoting a 'third way', New Labour has sought to confront this left/right dichotomy (see Leggett 2004). As Blair (1997) stated in his fore-word to Labour's manifesto for the 1997 General Election, 'We aim to put behind us the bitter political struggles of left and right that have torn our country apart for too many decades. Many of those conflicts have no rele-vance whatsoever to the modern world – public versus private, bosses versus workers, middle class versus working class' (p. 2).

The concept of the 'third way' (which has been applied to a variety of political movements, including 'Italian liberal socialism, European neo-fascism' and 'green political thought'; Bastow and Martin 2003: x) was chosen as a descriptor for this new approach. The constituent features of New Labour's 'third way' were fleshed out in subsequent publications by Blair (1998) and Giddens (1998).

In a Fabian pamphlet, Blair attempted to counter the charge that New Labour was a value-free zone by setting out four distinctive 'third way' values. Equal worth was the *first* such value. 'Social justice must be founded on the equal worth of each individual, whatever their background, capabil-ity, creed or race. Talent and effort should be encouraged to flourish in all quarters, and governments must act decisively to end discrimination and prejudice' (Blair 1998: 3). According to Blair, the *second* core 'third way' value, opportunity for all, 'has too often been neglected or distorted' by both the right, who have focused too narrowly on freeing individuals from coer-cive forms of state intervention, and the left, who have 'too readily down-played [the state's] duty to promote a wide range of responsibilities for individuals to advance themselves and their families' (p. 3). Responsibility is the *third* value identified by Blair. He contends that this value has for too long become the 'preserve of the Right' (p. 3). The 'third way' seeks to recon-nect rights with responsibilities. 'The rights we enjoy reflect the duties we owe: rights and opportunity without responsibility are engines of selfishness and greed' (p. 4). The *fourth* 'third way' value is community. For Blair, an acceptance of the need for strong government for the promotion of freedom does not mean that the community and voluntary activity should be margin-alized as it was by the left in the twentieth century. 'A key challenge of progressive politics is to use the state as an enabling force, protecting effective communities and voluntary organizations and encouraging their growth to tackle new needs, in partnership as appropriate' (p. 4).

In response to some initial criticism that New Labour's 'third way' approach was moving closer to the neo-liberal, rather than the social demo-cratic, end of the political spectrum both Blair and Giddens sought to high-light the progressive nature of the 'third way'. In an article in *Prospect* in 2001, Blair declared that New Labour's approach is 'not a third way between conservative and social democratic philosophy. It is social dem-ocracy renewed. It is firmly anchored in the tradition of progressive politics and the values which have motivated the democratic left for more than a century' (p. 10). Similarly, Giddens (2002) argued that 'the new social democracy seeks to preserve the basic values of the left – a belief in a solidarity and inclusive society, a commitment to combating inequality and protecting the vulnerable. It asserts that active government, coupled with strong public institutions and a developed welfare state, have an indispensable role to play in furthering these objectives. However, it holds that many traditional leftist perspectives or policies either no longer do so, or have become directly counterproductive' (p. 10).

Although this 'reincarnation' did not signify a retreat from the central tenets of the 'third way' thesis that had been previously advanced, it did represent a desire to position New Labour as a progressive left of centre political movement that wanted to combine the insights of new liberal thinkers such as T.H. Green, Beveridge and Keynes with some of the more traditional elements of social democracy (Blair 1999, 2002; see also Freeden 1999). 'In the last century, the tradition of social liberalism emphasized individual freedom in a market economy. Social democracy used the power of government to advance social justice. The third way works to combine their commitments in a relevant way for the 21st century' (Blair 2001: 10).

Whether New Labour's 'third way' can be equated with a modernized form of social democracy is open to question. The diverse and changing nature of social democracy over time makes it difficult to provide a definitive answer to this question (Pierson 2001). As Sassoon (1997) reminds us, social democracy has historically been equated with political movements seeking fundamental economic and social change along Marxist lines as well as with the more modest reformist agendas pursued by post-1945 western European parties which sought to humanize, rather than abolish capitalism. While social democracy has come to be almost universally regarded as a non-violent doctrine, following the decision by the German Social Democratic Party to heed Bernstein's advice and abandon the revolutionary road in the late nineteenth century, its other defining characteristics have proved more difficult to establish. As Gamble and Wright (1999) note, social democracy 'is not a particular historical programme or political party or interest group, or even an unchanging set of values. As a political movement its only fixed point is its constant search to build and sustain political majorities for reforms of economic and social institutions which counter injustice and reduce inequality' (p. 2). The problem with a broad definition of this kind is that the term social democracy could be applied to almost any government or society that adopts a 'programme of social amelioration' (Pierson 2001: 146) or which seeks to balance the conflicting interests of the market, the state, the individual and the community (see Veit-Wilson 2000, for a similar definitional debate concerning the welfare state).

Although not a static entity, social democracy has always tended to be linked with particular approaches or policies at particular points in time. In the second half of the twentieth century, for example, Western European social democracy was associated with Keynesian economic interventionism designed to secure full employment and economic growth, as well as redistributive forms of state welfare. Indeed, those North European nations, such as Sweden, which actively pursued such policies, came to be regarded as exemplars of social democratic nations or regimes (Esping-Andersen 1990).

It is New Labour's desire to move away from 'emblematic' means of this kind that has led some to question its social democratic credentials. As Gamble and Wright (1999) note, 'self-professed guardians of the social democratic tradition . . . believe that certain core ideas such as redistribution, universalist welfare and economic regulation, as well as the link between Labour and the trade unions, cannot be abandoned without abandoning social democracy itself' (p. 4).

According to New Labour, it is both desirable and necessary to deviate from some of these 'core ideas' given broader economic and social developments. Although they have, for example, adopted a different approach towards the welfare state in comparison to previous post-1945 Labour governments, New Labour maintains that it is still part of a modern social democratic movement.

New Labour and the Welfare State

New Labour's 'third way' welfare strategy has six inter-locking themes. First, it is argued that a modern welfare state should be *active*, rather than *passive*. In practice, this means that working age benefit recipients who are capable of undertaking paid work should be encouraged to return to the labour market in order to avoid the debilitating effects of long-term dependency on state benefits. As former Cabinet Minister David Blunkett (2001) contends, 'Paid work is the key to productive and fulfilling lives. Of course, there are many other worthwhile forms of fulfilment and contribution, not least unpaid parenting, but in modern societies, work is central to an individual's identity, their social status and their ability to exercise real choices in other areas of their lives' (p. 92).

Secondly, any remaining ideological preference for publicly provided welfare services should be abandoned. Giddens (2002), for example, suggests that the common good may be advanced by the increased involvement of 'mutuals, social enterprises, not-for-profit trusts and public benefit corporations' (p. 65). New Labour supports greater private sector involvement in both the financing and delivery of public services provided that it results in higher quality provision (Brown 2003). As New Labour has emphasized continually pragmatism rather than ideology is what matters

Thirdly, in a 'consumerist' age, the welfare state should, they suggest, be more responsive to the needs and preferences of service users. Although the public still want services such as education and health to be state funded, they also want individually tailored services that meet their needs and aspirations rather than the uniform and undifferentiated services of the past (see

Blair 2002). New providers or new configurations of existing services are seen as necessary to fulfil this goal. In addition, the rise of consumerism has led New Labour to distance itself from the idea that universal services must be defended by virtue of their propensity to enhance social cohesion (see Titmuss 1950, 1970). While contemporary citizens are not deemed to be devoid of interest in the well-being of their neighbours, they are no longer judged to derive additional satisfaction from the fact that the services they might receive are also available to others on the basis of common citizenship. This has led New Labour to the view that government should not defend the universal principle *per se*, but rather seek to provide services in ways (including selectivity) that best meet the perceived needs of self-interested consumers.

Fourthly, the key objective of a modern welfare state should be to extend opportunity in society by tackling socially constructed barriers to advancement such as poor schooling or inadequate health provision (Le Grand 1999; White 2001b), rather than by pursuing a more egalitarian distribution of income and wealth. As Gordon Brown (1999) contends, 'what people resent about Britain today is not that some people who have worked hard have done well. What angers people is that millions are denied the opportunity to realize their potential are powerless to do so. It is this inequality that must be addressed' (p. 42).

Fifthly, individuals should be expected to take more responsibility for their own welfare and to take an active part in their local community. In terms of the former, New Labour lays great stress on the need to match rights with responsibilities. Citizens are to be encouraged to adopt a more 'reciprocal' mindset in which state support is seen less as an unconditional right, but more like a 'gift' exchange. From this perspective, the receipt of government support in the shape of work, educational or training opportunities should be reciprocated by a readiness on the part of citizens to utilize such opportunities to the full. New Labour's positive response to the communitarian ideas of writers such as Macmurray (see Blair 1996b; Hale 2002; Prideaux 2005) and Etzioni (1997) also leads them to stress the importance of citizens taking a more active role in creating stronger, sustainable neighbourhoods. As Mandelson and Liddle (1996) suggest, 'New Labour emphatically do not seek to provide centralized "statist" solutions to every social and economic problem. Rather it aims to enable people to work together to achieve things for themselves and their fellow citizens' (p. 27).

Finally, the performance of publicly funded welfare services should be monitored to ensure that service users are provided with the highest possible standard of provision. Importantly, New Labour is sceptical of the claim that welfare professionals, motivated by a public service ethic, can be relied upon to develop high quality, cost efficient services without external monitoring (Le Grand 2003). From this perspective, a modern welfare state will only operate effectively if central government sets rigorous targets and establishes audit and inspection regimes.

Into power

New Labour's victory in the General Election of May 1997 provided an opportunity to put these principles into practice. Although this outcome was widely predicted, the margin of New Labour's success was enexpected. With 43% of the popular vote, New Labour secured 418 seats giving them an overall majority of 179 seats. New Labour proved 'remarkably successful at winning over English Conservative swing voters, especially in the marginal constituencies'. There was a decisive electoral switch to Labour across all social classes, age groups (except the over 65s), and genders (Driver and Martell 2006: 20). Further electoral success was achieved in 2001, when the lowest turnout in a General Election since 1918 (59.3%) failed to dent New Labour's electoral dominance. In this second 'landslide' victory 'only 21 out of 641 seats in mainland Britain changed hands' (Butler and Kavanagh 2002: 251). Labour secured 41% of the votes cast (412 seats), leaving it with an overall majority of 167 seats. Labour then went on to achieve an unprecedented third General Election victory in 2005. On a slightly higher turn out (61%), the Party secured just 35.2% of the popular vote, but this was still sufficient to leave it with an overall majority of 66 seats.

New Labour in practice: social policy under Blair – 1997–2007

New Labour's record on social policy can be examined from both an 'intrinsic' and 'extrinsic' perspective. As Powell (2002) explains, 'intrinsic evaluation examines performance in its own terms, with reference to stated goals. Extrinsic evaluation is based on a "third party" specification of criteria, and may result in criticizing a government for failing to achieve something that is not an objective, but which the third party thinks should be an objective' (p. 4). In reviewing New Labour's welfare record, this section will examine their achievements and shortcomings from an intrinsic perspective.

In his preface to the Labour Party's manifesto for the 2005 General Election, Tony Blair declared that:

> Our ideals are undimmed: extend opportunity to all, demand responsibility from all, secure justice for all. Our policies are refreshed; never has a governing party proposed a more wide-ranging programme of change for the country. Our vision is clear: a country more equal in its opportunities, more secure in its communities, more confident in the future. It is our social contract: we help you, you help yourself; you benefit and the country benefits.
>
> (Labour Party 2005: 9)

Although some might regard this vision as uninspiring (Collins 2003; Page 2007), it can be argued that New Labour has adopted a consistent approach to social policy since returning to government in 1997. It has sought to create an active welfare state, encourage diverse forms of provision, focus on the needs of consumers, expand opportunities for all, increase personal responsibility and enhance the level of provider accountability (see pp. 108–9). It is useful to look at each of these themes in turn.

An active Welfare State

New Labour signalled its intention to create an active welfare state by introducing a 'welfare-to-work' programme a year after their election victory in 1997. Funded by a windfall tax on the profits of the privatized utility companies, a 'flagship' New Deal scheme for young people under the age of 25 was introduced in 1998. Under this initiative, young people were first provided with assistance to help them find work. Those unable to secure a job after this initial stage were then provided with subsidized employment, full-time education or training, voluntary work or work with the Environmental Task Force. All young 'New Dealers' were denied the 'fifth option' of non-participation. Additional New Deal programmes were subsequently introduced. Most of these schemes, such as the New Deal for Lone Parents (1997), the New Deal for Disabled People (1998) and the New Deal 50+ (for those over the age of 50 in 1999) were voluntary in the first instance. Those covered by these schemes were offered advice and information about opportunities for paid work. In contrast those aged 25 or over who came within the remit of New Deal for the long-term unemployed were required to receive advice, and participate in job searches and training. Subsequently, the passage of the Welfare Reform and Pensions Act in 1999 paved the way for the introduction of compulsory, work-focused yearly interviews for lone parents (April 2001) and disabled people. By 2006 it was proposed that lone parents who had been claiming Income Support for over a year and whose youngest child was of secondary school age should be required to attend a work-focused interview every three months (Cm. 6730 2005).

New Labour recognized that a number of complementary measures were needed to smooth the transition from welfare to work and to provide clear financial incentives to return to the labour market. These included the introduction of a statutory minimum wage (1999), tax credits (a Working Families' Tax Credit was introduced in October 1999 and was eventually superseded by two separate tax credits, the Working Tax Credit and the Child Tax Credit in April 2003) and a National Childcare Strategy designed to increase the supply of affordable substitute care for children up to the age of 14.

Welfare to work has been an enduring feature of New Labour's 'active' welfare strategy since 1997 (Labour Party 1997, 2001, 2005). By the time of the 2005 General Election, for example, New Labour highlighted the need to reform Incapacity Benefit and enhance its Access to Work support scheme so that more people with disabilities could be encouraged to return to the labour market.

It is difficult to assess the impact of New Labour's welfare to work strategy given that the buoyancy of the economy is likely to have increased the demand for labour amongst the target groups. Nevertheless, there is some evidence to suggest that welfare to work has had some positive effects (Driver and Martell 2006). The labour market participation of lone parents, for example, rose from around 45% in 1997 to 55% in 2005 (see Gregg and Harness 2003; McKnight 2005). It remains to be seen, though, whether welfare to work schemes will prove effective in helping those with low skill levels or those whose personal circumstances make it difficult to find, or retain, a job.

Diverse welfare provision

As part of its drive for 'innovation and service improvement' (Blair 2002: 14), New Labour has been keen to encourage the private sector and voluntary bodies to provide publicly-funded services. This has been particularly noticeable in the areas of health and education. In both of these spheres, New Labour has expanded the Private Finance Initiative introduced by the previous Conservative government in order to finance its hospital and school building programme through 'Public-Private Partnerships'. Under this scheme, a private sector contractor finances and builds a new hospital or school, which is then leased back to the public sector. In addition to the defrayed costs of such projects, the government benefits from the fact that these schemes have been 'designed to transfer risk for construction delays and cost over-runs away from the taxpayer and towards private sector companies who have strong incentives as well as specialist skills to manage those risks' (p. 14).

New Labour's enthusiasm for private sector involvement has also extended to direct service provision. In the case of health care, Alan Milburn, who replaced Frank Dobson as the Health Secretary in 1998, agreed a 'concordat' with the Independent Health Care Association in 2000 guaranteeing private health providers a share of NHS funding for routine procedures (Toynbee and Walker 2001). Private sector companies have also taken on the role previously performed by local education authorities in two 'under-performing' inner London Boroughs, Hackney and Islington, as well as in northern towns and cities, such as Leeds, Rotherham and Sheffield (see Bochel 2005). Private contractors were also invited to run two 'sub-standard' schools in Surrey.

New Labour has encouraged the expansion of 'independent', state-funded, faith-based schools 'on the grounds that they have achieved high attainment levels for their pupils' (Labour Party 2005: 37). Under the Education Act of 2006 the subsidies for faith schools were extended. New Labour also paved the way for the development of 'independent' City Academy schools in deprived areas of the country under the Learning and Skills Act of 2000. Some 200 such schools are due to be opened by 2010. Under this scheme sponsors who agree to make a capital investment of around £2 million gain effective control over the curriculum and the admissions policy of the new school (Beckett 2005). Even those publicly-funded schools and hospitals that remain in the state sector have been encouraged to adopt a more 'individualized' ethos. New Labour wants all secondary schools, for example, to become independent specialist schools 'with a strong ethos, high quality leadership, good discipline (including school uniforms), setting by ability and high-quality facilities as the norm' (Labour Party 2005: 35). Although all of these schools will follow the National Curriculum, they will also have distinctive Centres of Excellence in one or two subjects.

In the case of health, all NHS hospitals and Primary Care Trusts can, since the passage of the Health and Social Care Act of 2003, apply to an independent regulator to be granted foundation status. Although these Trusts will remain formally within the NHS and will not be able to impose charges on NHS patients or exceed the existing resource share derived from private patients, they will 'be free to set their own pay scales, borrow on the private market, enter into contracts with private providers, and determine their own priorities' (Pollock 2004: 71).

New Labour's enthusiasm for diverse forms of provision has also been evident in the area of housing. It has shown little inclination to return to the traditional provider role of local authorities favouring instead a diverse mix of social landlords. Voluntary stock transfer from local authorities to registered social landlords increased from 22,248 dwellings in 1996/97 to over 132,360 in 2000/01 (Wilcox 2002). Councils with a 'good' record of housing management have also been allowed to set up arm's length management organizations (ALMOs) under which a board comprising tenants, councillors and community representatives manages the housing stock. Unlike voluntary stock transfer, an ALMO can be created without balloting existing tenants.

New Labour has undoubtedly succeeded in encouraging a more diverse range of publicly-funded welfare providers, although it has not always proved easy to find new sponsors or agencies willing to become involved in this way (see Smithers 2005). It remains difficult, however, to determine whether any improvement in service quality resulting from a change of provider is a reflection of organizational reform or the enhanced resources that many of these new providers received (Toynbee and Walker 2005).

Consumer focused

New Labour's approach to social policy has focused on the needs of service users, rather than providers. This has resulted in a number of significant changes in the organization and delivery of state welfare services.

In education, New Labour has, for example, responded to parental concerns about the poor standard of teaching in some state schools by introducing the School Standards and Education Act in 1998, which empowered the government to close poorly performing schools and to dispatch 'improvement' teams to 'under achieving' LEAs. A 'Fresh Start' scheme was introduced under which a 'failing' school could be closed and then re-opened under the direction of a new head teacher and governors. Like their Conservative predecessors New Labour has continued to publish school performance league tables on the grounds that parents will be unable to make informed choices about their child's prospective schooling without such information. The best performing schools have been awarded 'Beacon' status to signify their capacity both to deliver high quality education and to offer help and support to less successful schools.

The decision by New Labour's first Education Secretary, David Blunkett, to reappoint Chris Woodhead as Chief Inspector of Schools, despite his unpopularity with the teaching unions, was also indicative of the government's desire to support those who had demonstrated a commitment to service users rather than providers. The establishment of a General Teaching Council in 2000 was an attempt to raise teaching standards, which were also to be enhanced by the introduction of performance-related pay.

In the area of health care, New Labour has endeavoured to cut waiting times for NHS outpatient and inpatient appointments. In its General Election manifesto of 2005 the government claimed that inpatient appointment times had been cut from 18 to 9 months since 1997. They promised to ensure that by the end of 2008 no patient would wait for more than 18 weeks 'from the time they are referred for a hospital operation by their GP until the time they have that operation' (Labour Party 2005: 58). By the end of 2008 patients undergoing non-urgent hospital treatments will be able to choose any approved health care provider for their operation. Under an Expert Patients Programme, many patients with chronic conditions will also be provided with an opportunity to 'take control of their own care plans' (p. 64).

New Labour has also attempted to make the NHS more responsive to the needs of the consumer by introducing a number of innovative services. These include NHS Direct (a telephone advice service that dealt with 6.4 million calls in 2004), NHS Online (a website that had 6.5 million 'hits' in the same year) and over 40 NHS walk-in centres (Toynbee and Walker 2005). These are due to be complemented in the future by the development of 'new specialized diagnostic and testing services; comprehensive out of hours services; high street drop-in centres for chiropody, physiotherapy and check-ups' (Labour

Party 2005: 61). Part of the remit of the National Institute for Clinical Excellence (NICE), which was established in 1999, was to ensure that all patients had access to high quality care. In addition, an independent Commission for Health Improvement was created with powers to inspect hospitals and monitor service performance. Finally, the decision to allow 'high performing' acute and specialist hospital trusts to opt for greater autonomy by applying for foundation status was also intended to make these organizations more responsive to consumer demands (Allsop and Baggott 2004).

New Labour has striven to ensure that all state-funded providers focus on improving the quality of services they are contracted to deliver. To this end, it has introduced a series of measures that aim, for example, to improve the quality of education in failing schools and to ensure that patients can access the medical services they need more easily and speedily. Time will tell whether this consumerist approach will leads to long-term improvements in educational achievements or 'healthier' citizens.

Opportunities for all

Opportunity enhancement has been a central feature of New Labour's welfare strategy since 1997. Improving opportunities, particularly for labour market participation, has been seen as a vital means of enhancing both individual and collective well-being (Cm. 4445 1999). Policy has focused in particular on ensuring that every child has the opportunity to develop their potential. Poverty and sub-standard education have been identified as two central barriers to the achievement of this goal.

According to one government statistical series (Department of Social Security 1997, 2001) poverty was blighting the lives of a third of all children in 1999/2000 compared with just 12.6% in 1979. In response to this, the Prime Minister took the bold step of promising, in a lecture he delivered at Toynbee Hall in March 1999, to abolish child poverty within 20 years (Blair 1999).

This was to be achieved in various ways, including through the generic measures designed to improve parental income levels such as welfare to work and tax credits. The Working Families Tax Credit scheme, which included a childcare element, was expected to increase the average income of recipients by £31/week more than the Family Credit scheme it replaced in 2000/2001 (Cm. 4865 2000). Child Benefit (which can be claimed by all families with dependent children) and children's allowances for those receiving Income Support were also increased substantially during the first three terms of the Labour government (see Stewart 2005).

Other measures designed to improve the position of children included a national parenting helpline and the Sure Start programme. Introduced in April 1999, some 250 Sure Start schemes (rising to 522 by 2004) were established in the most deprived neighbourhoods in the UK, providing health and support services, such as day centres for the under 4s and their parents. Like the pioneering Head Start programme in the US, it was hoped that this scheme would enable poorer children to flourish once they started their mainstream schooling.

Many of New Labour's educational reforms have been designed to ensure that all children have opportunities to develop their academic potential. These included a guaranteed, free part-time nursery place for all 4-year-olds from 2000 and for all 3-year-olds from 2004. Compulsory one-hour daily teaching periods devoted to literacy (1998) and numeracy (1999) were also introduced. In keeping with one of its first-term manifesto commitments, the average class sizes for the 5–7 age groups was reduced to below thirty (funds for this initiative came from the abolition of the Conservatives' assisted places scheme).

Labour has introduced a number of special initiatives to tackle low pupil achievement in deprived areas of the country. These have included the setting up of 73 Education Action Zones in 1999 and 2000. In each of these zones, a cluster of two or three secondary schools and the 'feeder' primary schools from which they drew their pupils collaborated with local businesses and other local organizations to create more positive and rewarding educational outcome for children. A subsequent scheme, *Excellence in Cities* (Department for Education and Employment [DfEE] 1999), has been providing targeted support for secondary school pupils aged from 11 to 16 in 58 disadvantaged urban LEAs. As McKnight *et al.* (2005) make clear, this is 'a more prescriptive programme, with specific funding available for particular purposes, namely employing learning mentors, making provision for gifted and talented pupils and providing learning support units and City Learning Centres' (p. 55). An Education Maintenance Allowance scheme was introduced in 1999. This initiative aims to encourage student from low income families to remain in full-time education by providing them with an allowance of up to £40/week.

New Labour has also endeavoured to increase the numbers of young people in higher education, where a participation rate of 50% by 2010 remains the long-term goal (Labour Party 2005). In order to help meet the rising costs of higher student numbers New Labour, in line with one of the recommendations of the Dearing Report on *Higher Education in the Learning Society* (National Council of Inquiry into Higher Education, 1997), decided to introduce university student tuition fees under the Teaching and Higher Education Act of 1998. The ending of free tuition was justified on the grounds that students would be able to recoup the costs through the higher lifetime earnings that graduates could command. The method of recouping fee income has since been modified from an unpopular up-front system to a post-graduation repayment scheme. Under the 2004 Higher Education Act, students from poorer families are eligible for reduced fees and a maintenance grant worth at least £2700 per annum (Driver and Martell 2006).

Finally, New Labour has introduced what has been described as 'an entirely new "pillar" of welfare policy in the form of asset based welfare' (Harker 2005: 267). A Child Trust scheme was introduced in the autumn of 2002 to provide all children with a 'nest egg' when they reach adulthood. Each child receives a lump sum payment, which can be topped up by relatives or (in the case of poorer children) by the state. The fund can be accessed at the age of 18 and used for a designated purpose, such as helping to fund continuing education or training (see Nissan and Le Grand 2000).

New Labour has made steady progress in relation to opportunity enhancement though it acknowledges that more needs to be done (Labour Party 2005). Despite a promising start in its attack on child poverty (Department of Social Security 2001; Piachaud 2001; Sutherland *et al.* 2003), New Labour failed to reach its initial benchmark target of reducing child poverty by 25% by 2004–05. Although there were 700,000 fewer children in poverty by this date compared with 1998–99, this represented a fall of only 17% (based on the government's own poverty measure of less than 60% of median household income before housing costs; the figure increased to 23% after housing costs). According to Palmer *et al.* (2006), it remains the case that, despite all New Labour's efforts to date, the alleviation of poverty is difficult to achieve unless both parents are in paid work.

New Labour can point to improvements in educational attainment at both Key Stage One (age 7) and Key Stage Two (age 11), and a narrowing of the educational achievements of 'poor' schools (in which 40% of pupils qualify for free school meals) vis-a-vis 'rich' schools (in which 5% or less of pupils are eligible for free school meals; see McKnight *et al.* 2005). The position in secondary schools is, however, less encouraging (Palmer *et al.* 2006). Although 88% of 16-year-olds now obtain five passes at General Certificate of Secondary Education (GCSE), the proportion achieving 'good' grades (grade C or above) has hovered at around 57% in recent years, falling to 44% if English and Mathematics are included (2005–06). Despite the fact that the number of pupils leaving school without any qualifications has fallen to around 5%, this group contains disproportionately high numbers of pupils from poorer backgrounds (McKnight *et al.* 2005). In respect of their goals for higher education, it is too early to judge whether New Labour's reforms will help or hinder the recruitment of larger numbers of students from poorer backgrounds (see Callender 2003).

Increased personal responsibility

Given its belief that in an era of globalization the state is no longer able to provide a guaranteed level of 'social' security for all, New Labour has encouraged citizens to assume greater responsibility for maintaining their own well-being. Accordingly, citizens have been encouraged to remain in full-time education, acquire new skills, follow a healthy lifestyle and make appropriate arrangements for old age.

Young people who receive an Educational Maintenance Allowance, for example, are expected to attend school. Failure to do so can result in a financial penalty such as the loss of a 'graduation' bonus. Under the School Standards and Framework Act of 1998, the parents of school-age children have been expected to sign a home-school agreement under which they promise to ensure that their child attends school regularly and to support the school's homework policy (see Halpern *et al.* 2004). Those parents deemed to make inadequate efforts to prevent their child from truanting face the prospect of a fine or, in extreme cases, imprisonment.

This emphasis on personal responsibility has been particularly evident in New Labour's approach to anti-social behaviour and criminal justice. While it remains committed to tackling the underlying causes of crime and helping communities deal with crime, New Labour has distanced itself from the 'Labour approach of the past' by refusing to excuse criminal or anti-social acts on the grounds of material or other forms of disadvantage (Labour Party 1997). In an attempt to tackle rising levels of crime and disorder, especially amongst young people and to meet the needs of the law abiding majority for safer communities, New Labour has reformed the juvenile justice system, introduced anti-social behaviour orders and legislated for the imposition of curfews for young people in designated areas. The parents of young offenders can also be issued with a parenting order, under which they will be provided with guidance and counselling (Randall 2004).

In 2007, New Labour announced the creation of 40 'respect' zones. Under this initiative councils, in areas such as Blackpool, Exeter, Leeds and Newcastle, who have demonstrated their resolve to tackle anti-social behaviour, have been granted additional funds to extend their work in this field. In one of these areas, Bolton, a range of measures has been employed to tackle this issue including anti-social behaviour orders, voluntary 'acceptable behaviour' contracts and intensive support for those families that are at risk of being made homeless because of their conduct (*The Guardian*, 23 January 2007).

New Labour has emphasized the need for all citizens to take greater responsibility for their personal well-being and to become active members of their local community. This reflects New Labour's belief that the government is no longer able, if it ever could, to provide citizens with a guaranteed level of security and well-being. It is extremely difficult to measure how successful the government has been in this endeavour. A number of 'outputs' can be identified, such as the backing it has given to local councils who offer residents the chance to engage in their local neighbourhood so that 'social inclusion and mutual support' can flourish (Cm. 6673 2005: 51). The government has also encouraged individuals to take responsibility for their own behaviour and for the conduct of their dependants. It is difficult, though, to assess whether the level of personal responsibility has increased in society. Verifiable declines in crime, anti-social behaviour and drug misuse might eventually come to be regarded as indicators of the effectiveness of New Labour's 'responsibility enhancing' measures.

Setting targets and monitoring performance

One distinctive feature of New Labour's welfare strategy has been the introduction of targets for welfare providers. Public Service Agreement with accompanying SMART (specific, measurable, achievable, relevant, timed) targets were put in place, for example, in an effort to reassure the Treasury that the state was getting a 'maximum bang for its buck' (Toynbee and Walker 2001: 103). Some of New Labour's targets relate to highly specific objectives such as reducing deaths from cancer and heart disease, raising literacy and numeracy levels, or cutting street crime and rough sleeping. Others, in contrast, have been devised to monitor the performance of public bodies such as local authorities. During New Labour's second term, the Audit Commission was charged with constructing Comprehensive Perform- ance Assessments, ranging from excellent to poor, for all local councils in England and Wales on the basis of existing reports and performance indicators (Travers 2005: 76).

One of the reasons that the Blair governments have been wedded to tar- gets is because they encourage service providers to focus on outcomes. According to Mulgan (2005), 'poor people, who have traditionally had to make do with poor services, have been the main beneficiaries of tighter performance management (as the relative performance of schools, hospitals and police forces in poorer areas has risen faster than average) and are likely to continue to be the main beneficiaries as government makes more use of floor standards and guaranteed minimums' (p. 100).

Although New Labour's commitment to targets and performance man- agement has not wavered during the Blair era, this has not precluded it from adjusting these measures in the light of experience. Local Public Service Agreements and Local Area Agreements have been introduced, for example, in recognition of the fact that the achievement of national targets often requires collaboration between councils, health authorities, businesses and the voluntary sector at the local level.

Since coming to power in 1997, New Labour has been keen to provide the public with information about its expressed policy goals and the progress it has made in fulfilling these and the areas where further improvement is needed. For example, the Green Paper, *New Ambitions for our Country: a New Contract for Welfare*, published in 1998 (Cm. 3805 1998) outlined New Labour's welfare objectives and the associated measures of success. In order to demonstrate its commitment to public accountability, New Labour has, since 1999, published a series of annual reports entitled *Opportunity for All* (Cm. 4445 1999), which track the progress that it has made in tackling poverty and social exclusion. According to their Seventh Annual Report (Cm. 6673 2005), improvements were noted in two-thirds of their sixty selected indicators since 1997, including the situation of children in workless households, employment rates of lone parents and rough sleepers. No change was observed in relation to seven other indicators while a deteriorating position was found in a further seven indicators including childhood obesity, families in temporary accommodation and employment for those with few qualifications. (An assessment could not be made in relation to the five other indicators because of the lack of reliable evidence; see also Palmer *et al.* 2003.)

Overall, then, New Labour has succeeded in creating a target culture and has set about monitoring the extent to which these goals have been achieved. Although there have been some measurable improvements in 'performance', it is often difficult to determine how far this is a result of target setting or other factors. Moreover, it has been acknowledged that the focus on specific targets can, especially when additional resources or benefits are awarded to those who meet these objectives, lead to the neglect of other 'non-measured' parts of the service.

Investing in the Welfare State

New Labour's initial determination to secure a reputation for economic 'prudence' (Keegan 2003) by such means as granting independence to the Bank of England over monetary policy (just days after their election victory in 1997) and adhering to the short-term spending plans of the previous Conservative government, led to concerns amongst some party members about the government's commitment to the welfare state. Indeed, the decision to press ahead with Conservative plans to abolish One Parent Benefit and the lone parent premium attached to Income Support in 1997 led to the government's first backbench revolt (Purdy 2000). A more expansionary phase followed, however, after the Comprehensive Spending Review of 2000. Steady growth, low inflation and falling unemployment created the conditions for sustained investment in welfare services such as health and education. Although this major expansion was not planned to last beyond 2008, the extent of New Labour's investment should not be underestimated. During the first term of the New Labour government, real term spending on the NHS increased by 4.8% per year rising to 7.4% per year during the second term. By 2007/08 it is estimated that 9% of Gross Domestic Product will be devoted to NHS spending compared with 6.5% in 2000 (Glennerster 2005). Given New Labour's focus on outcomes, this spending has been linked with such measures as speedier appointment times with GPs, reduced waiting times for hospital treatment and a maximum 4-hour wait in an accident and emergency unit.

It is clear that New Labour's investment has led to measurable improve-ments in *outputs* such as increased numbers of better-paid doctors and nurses and speedier appointments time. Whether such investment will lead to improved *outcomes* such as fewer premature deaths from cancer and heart disease is yet to be determined.

New Labour: still a force for 'progressive' social policy and a more equal society?

Many extrinsic critics of New Labour have been concerned about the degree to which the Blair governments have been pursuing a progressive policy agenda. Indeed many of the backbench revolts faced by the New Labour government (Cowley 2005) reflect anxiety about the Party's long-term commitment to the welfare state and the creation of a more equal society. Four specific concerns have been raised about the direction of New Labour's social policy.

First, the assertion that greater private sector or voluntary sector involve-ment in the delivery of public services poses no threat to the underlying ethos of state welfare has been challenged. According to Marquand (1999):

> In the public domain, goods should not be treated as commodities or proxy commodities. The language of buyer and seller, producer and customer, does not belong in the public domain and nor do the relation-ships which that language implies. Doctors and nurses do not 'sell' medical services; students are not 'customers' of their teachers; police-man and policewomen do not 'produce' public order. The attempt to force these relationships into a market mould undermines the service ethic, hollows out the institutions that embody them and robs the notion of common citizenship of part of its meaning.
>
> (p. 15)

Secondly, New Labour's belief that a twenty-first-century welfare state must respond to the public as discerning consumers rather than as 'selfless' citizens who value the fact that the services they receive are also available to others on the basis of common citizenship, rather than ability to pay, has also been questioned. While some such as Reisman (1977) have always been sceptical as to whether the cross-class bonds of 'brotherhood and friendship' developed in a National Health Service hospital ward could survive the 'disintegrative differentials in pay, power, prestige, security and facilities' (p. 111) in the competitive world outside, others have maintained that solidarity can be enhanced in this way (Titmuss 1950, 1970; Lawson 2005). Certainly, such solidarity is unlikely to flourish if service users are encour-aged to focus exclusively on their own well-being rather than the position of their neighbours (Schwartz 2005). If a neighbourhood school closes because a number of parents have exercised their 'right' to send their children to a school further afield, the costs will be borne by those who wanted their children to be educated locally (Benn and Millar 2005). As Lipsey (2005) contends, 'when everyone in the public sector tries to maximize their personal choice through the exercise of individual choice, it may have unpredictable consequences on institutions like schools and hospitals. The effect may be to give people less of what they want' (p. 27; see Le Grand 2005 for a contrary view).

Thirdly, although New Labour's efforts to improve opportunities for specific groups in society, such as lone parents and their children have been welcomed, the government has been criticized for their reluctance to tackle the overall growth of inequality (see Hills and Stewart 2005b) by means of more progressive income and wealth taxes. Criticism has also been levelled at New Labour for failing to counter the advantages that accrue to privately educated pupils in terms of gaining access to the most prestigious universities and to better-paid positions in the job market (see Collins 2001; Brighouse 2000).

Fourthly, New Labour's decision to link 'good' citizenship with labour market participation has proved disappointing to those who contend that a more progressive approach is needed to combat gender inequalities and to achieve a better 'work-home' balance (Williams 2001). By prioritizing work-based citizenship, New Labour has come to be seen as diminishing the worth of those who are unable to undertake paid work because of ill health or caring responsibilities. Although New Labour has improved the living standards of those whom it considers are genuinely unable to undertake paid work, such as older people, it has been reluctant to support those who might prefer a subsidized form of citizenship based on voluntary activity in their local community or caring for others. For New Labour, paid work is always to be preferred because it enhances personal esteem, creates opportunities for career advancement and provides an appropriate role model for children and young people. While New Labour has implemented a number of European Union directives relating to working hours and parental leave, its support for such measures has, according to May (2001), been based more on the opportunities it provides for flexible working and increased productivity, rather than its potential to redress gender divisions.

In its defence, New Labour supporters have maintained that a failure to adjust policy in the light of economic, social and demographic change in an era where support for progressive forms of social policy is 'conditional' at best, could result in less 'enlightened' policies coming to the fore (see Hills 2001; Sefton 2003). By responding positively to change, New Labour believes that it will be in a better position to *shape* policy in a more progressive way over the longer term. According to Gould (1998), with a New Labour government in office 'more poverty will be removed and more real change implemented than could ever be achieved by short, sharp, occasional spasms of radicalism' (p. 394).

Whether it is possible for a government to embrace the market and promote consumerism and diversity and still act in a progressive way in a 'post-ideological' world is open to question (Kellner 2003: 10). While New Labour has adopted a progressive stance in relation to child and pensioner poverty and in enhancing opportunities for disadvantaged groups (Toynbee and Walker 2001, 2005; Hills and Stewart 2005b; Pearce and Paxton 2005), it has shown little or no inclination to counter growing inequalities of income or wealth, increasingly insecure forms of employment or oppressive forms of managerialism within public sector organizations. It could be argued that New Labour's failure to address these issues at the current time is part of an 'accommodation to shape' strategy that is premised on the belief that such developments will take a considerable time to reverse (Smith 2004).

There is little sign, however, that New Labour is preparing a progressive accommodation to shape strategy of this kind (Taylor-Gooby 2000). Rather, it has adopted a non-socialist welfare strategy where the task of social policy is to complement rather than challenge market imperatives. The rolling programme of consumerist welfare reforms that have been introduced are intended to ensure that economic prosperity is promoted and not jeopardized by social policy. Labour, in its new guise, is not seeking to engender deep-rooted public support for the socialist transformation of society. Instead, it has based its electoral appeal on a professed ability to help citizens come to terms with global economic and social change, by encouraging them to acquire the skills and attitudes deemed necessary to succeed in this more dynamic environment. New Labour, it appears, wants to create a contended and ordered society in which substantial inequalities in income and wealth persist, but where the opportunities to obtain such rewards are extended. This represents a significant change from the transformative democratic socialist vision of previous post-1945 Labour governments. As such it will not resonate with many traditional Labour supporters. It has, however, much more in common with the 'revisionist' Conservative Party led by David Cameron, who has distanced himself from the Thatcher legacy by adopting a more compassionate attitude towards the poor and a more supportive approach to welfare spending (Cameron 2007; O'Hara 2007). Might we finally be witnessing the first ideological concensus between the two major parties not just about the role of the welfare state but also, more broadly, about the constituent features of the good society?

Further reading

Informative, although far from uniform, accounts of the metamorphosis of 'Old' Labour into New Labour are provided by Jones (1996), Shaw (1996), White

(2001a), Fielding (2003a), Finlayson (2003), Leggett (2005) and Bevir (2005). Influential 'insider' accounts of New Labour's approach include Mandelson and Liddle (1996), Blair (1998, 2002), Gould (1998), and Giddens (1998, 2000, 2002). A number of important articles and commentaries on New Labour are to be found in Chadwick and Heffernan's (2003) edited collection. Toynbee and Walker (2001; 2005), Powell (2002), Ludlam and Smith (2004), Seldon and Kavanagh (2005), Stewart and Hills (2005a) and Driver and Martell (2006) review New Labour's approach to social policy and offer initial assessments of their record in government.

Bibliography

Abel-Smith, B. (1958) Whose welfare state? in N. Mackenzie (ed.) *Conviction*. London: MacGibbon & Kee: 55–73.

Abel-Smith, B. and Townsend, P. (1965) *The Poor and the Poorest*. London: Bell & Sons.

Addison, P. (1977) *The Road to 1945*. London: Jonathan Cape.

Addison, P. (1992) *Churchill on the Home Front 1900–1955*. London: Jonathan Cape.

Adelman, P. (1986) *The Rise of the Labour Party 1800–1945*, 2nd edn. Harlow: Longman.

Adonis, A. (1997) New Labour, new plutocracy, old poor, *The Observer*, 7 August 1997.

Allsop, J. and Baggott, R. (2004) The NHS in England: from modernisation to marketisation? in N. Ellison, L. Bauld and M. Powell (eds) *Social Policy Review 16*. Bristol: Policy: 29–44.

Audit Commission (1986) *Making a Reality of Community Care*. London: HMSO.

Bacon, R. and Eltis, W. (1976) *Britain's Economic Problems: Too Few Producers*. London: Macmillan.

Bailey, B. (1995) James Chuter Ede and the 1944 Education Act, *History of Education*, 23(3): 209–20.

Ball, S. (2003) The Conservatives in opposition, 1906–79: a comparative analysis, in M. Garnett and P. Lynch (eds) *The Conservatives in Crisis*. Manchester: Manchester University Press: 7–28.

Barnett, C. (1986) *The Audit of War*. London: Macmillan.

Bastow, S. and Martin, J. (2003) *Third Way Discourse*. Edinburgh: Edinburgh University Press.

Beckett, C. and Beckett, F. (2004) *Bevan*. London: Haus.

Beckett, F. (2000) *Clem Attlee*. London: Politico's.

Beckett, F. (2005) Blair's flagships schools and the money that never was, *New Statesman*, 17 January 2005: 28–9.

Beer, S. (1965) *Modern British Politics*. London: Faber and Faber.

Bell, M., Butler, E., Marsland, D. and Pirie, M. (1994) *The End of the Welfare State*. London: Adam Smith Institute.

Benn, M. and Millar, F. (2005) First on our list, a good local school – and for all our children, *The Guardian*, 15 January 2005.

Bevan, A. (1978) *In Place of Fear*. London: Quartet.

Bevir, M. (2005) *New Labour A Critique*. London: Routledge.

Black, A. and Brooke, S.J. (1997) The Labour Party, women and the problem of gender, 1951–66, *Historical Journal*, 37(1): 173–98.

Black, J. (2004) *Britain Since the Seventies*. London: Reaktion.

Black, L. (2003a) *The Political Culture of the Left in Affluent Britain, 1951–64*. Basingstoke: Palgrave Macmillan.

Black, L. (2003b) What kind of people are you? Labour, the people and the 'new political history' in J. Callaghan, S. Fielding and S. Ludlam (eds) *Interpreting the Labour Party*. Manchester: Manchester University Press: 23–38.

Blair, T. (1995a) The power of the message, in P. Richards (ed.) (2004) *Tony Blair in His Own Words*. London: Politico's.

Blair, T. (1995b) Let us face the future: the 1945 anniversary lecture, in P. Richards, (ed.) (2004) *Tony Blair in His Own Words*. London: Politico's.

Blair, T. (1996a) Introduction: my vision for Britain, in G. Radice (ed.) *What Needs to Change*. London: HarperCollins: 3–17.

Blair, T. (1996b) Foreword, in P. Conford (ed.) *The Personal World: John Macmurray on Self and Society*. London: Floris.

Blair, T. (1997) Britain will be better with new Labour, foreword to Labour Party (1997), *New Labour Because Britain Deserves Better, The Labour Party Manifesto for the 1997 General Election*. London: Labour Party: 1–5.

Blair, T. (1998) *The Third Way*, Fabian Pamphlet 588. London: Fabian Society.

Blair, T. (1999) Beveridge revisited: a welfare state for the 21st century, in R. Walker (ed.) *Ending Child Poverty*. Bristol: Policy: 7–18.

Blair. T. (2001) 'Third way, phase two', *Prospect*, 61, March: 10–13.

Blair, T. (2002) *The Courage of our Convictions: Why Reform of the Public Services is the Route to Social Justice*. London: Fabian Society.

Blake, R. (1998) *The Conservative Party from Peel to Major*. London: Arrow.

Blunkett, D. (2001) *Politics and Progress*. London: Politico's.

Bochel, H. (2005) Education, in H. Bochel, C. Bochel, R. Page and R. Sykes (eds) *Social Policy: Issues and Developments*. Harlow: Pearson: 87–108.

Boxer, A. (1996) *The Conservative Governments 1951–64*. London: Longman.

Boyson, R. (1978) *Centre Forward: a Radical Conservative Programme*. London: Temple Smith.

Bridgen, P. and Lowe, R. (1998) *Welfare Policy Under the Conservatives 1951–1964*. London: Public Record Office.

Brighouse, H. (2000) *A Level Playing Field: the Reform of Private Schools*, Policy Report No. 52. London: Fabian Society.

Brivati, B. (1996) *Hugh Gaitskell*. London: Richard Cohen.

Brivati, B. (1997) Earthquake or watershed? Conclusions on New Labour in power, in B. Brivati and T. Bale (eds) *New Labour in Power*. London: Routledge: 183–99.

Brooke, S. (1992) *Labour's War: the Labour Party During the Second World War*. Oxford: Clarendon.

Brooke, S. (1995) (ed) *Reform and Reconstruction: Britain After the War, 1945–51*. Manchester: Manchester University Press.

Brown, G. (1999) Equality – then and now, in D. Leonard (ed.) *Crosland and New Labour*. Basingstoke: Macmillan: 35–48.

Brown, G. (2003) State and market: towards a public interest test, *Political Quarterly*, 7(3): 266–84.

Bruce, M. (1961) *The Coming of the Welfare State*. London: Basford.

Butler, D. and Kavanagh, D. (2002) *The British General Election of 2001*. Basingstoke: Palgrave.

Cairncross, A.K. (1985) *Years of Recovery: British Economic Policy, 1945–51*. London: Routledge.

Calder, A. (1971) *The People's War*. London: Panther.

Calder, A. (1992) *The Myth of the Blitz*. London: Pimlico.

Callender, C. (2003) Student financial support in higher education: access and exclusion, in M. Tight (ed.) *Access and Exclusion: International Perspectives on Higher Education Research*. London: Elsevier.

Cameron, D. (2007) No one will be left behind in a Tory Britain, *The Observer*, 27 January 2007: 31.

Campbell, J. (1993) *Edward Heath: a Biography*. London: Jonathan Cape.

Campbell, J. (1994) *Nye Bevan: a Biography*. London: Hodder & Stoughton.

Campbell, J. (2000) *Margaret Thatcher, Volume One: the Grocer's Daughter*. London: Jonathan Cape.

Campbell, J. (2003) *Margaret Thatcher, Volume Two: the Iron Lady*. London: Jonathan Cape.

Central Statistical Office (1995) *Fighting With Figures*. London: Central Statistical Office.

Chadwick, A. and Heffernan, R. (2003) Introduction: the New Labour phenomenon, in A. Chadwick and R. Heffernan (eds) *The New Labour Reader*. Cambridge: Polity.

Charmley, J. (1996) *A History of Conservative Politics, 1900–1996*. Basingstoke: Macmillan.

Childs, D. (2001) *Britain since 1945*, 5th edn. London: Routledge.

Clarke, P. (1978) *Liberals and Social Democrats*. London: Macmillan.

Clarke, P. (1996) *Hope and Glory Britain: 1900–1990*. London: Allen Lane.

Clarke, P. (2002) *The Cripps Version*. London: Allen Lane.

Cm. 555 (1988) *Working for Patients*. London: HMSO.

Cm. 1986 (1992) *The Health of the Nation*. London: HMSO.

Cm. 3425 (1996) *The National Health Service: a Service with Ambitions*. London: Stationery Office.

Cm. 3805 (1998) *New Ambitions for our Country: a New Contract for Welfare*. London: Stationery Office.

Cm. 3807 (1997) *The New NHS: Modern Dependable*. London: Stationery Office.

Cm. 4445 (1999) *Opportunity for all*, First Annual Report 1999. London: Stationery Office.

Cm. 4865 (2000) *Opportunity for all – One year on: Making a Difference*, Second Annual Report 2000. London: Stationery Office.

Cm. 6673 (2005) *Opportunity for all*, Seventh Annual Report 2005. London: Stationery Office.

Cm. 6730 (2005) *A New Deal for Welfare: Empowering People to Work*. London: Stationery Office.

Cmd. 6404 (1942) *Social Insurance and Allied Services*, The Beveridge Report. London: HMSO.

Cmd. 6502 (1944) *A National Health Service*. London: HMSO.

Cmd. 6527 (1944) *Employment Policy*. London: HMSO.

Cmd. 9333 (1953) *Report of the Phillips Committee on the Economic and Financial Problems of Provision for Old Age*. London: HMSO.

Cmd. 9663 (1956) *Report of the Committee into the Cost of the National Health Service*. London: HMSO.

Cmnd. 5174 (1972) *Education: a Framework for Expansion*. London: HMSO.

Cmnd. 7746 (1979) *The Government's Expenditure Plans 1980–81*. London: HMSO.

Cmnd. 9517 (1985) *The Reform of Social Security*. London: HMSO.

Cmnd. 9524 (1985) *Development of Higher Education in the 1990s*. London: HMSO.

Cmnd. 9771 (1986) *Primary Health Care: an Agenda for Discussion*. London: HMSO.

Coates, D. (1975) *The Labour Party and the Struggle for Socialism*. Cambridge: Cambridge University Press.

Coates, D. and Lawler, P. (eds) (2000) *New Labour in Power*. Manchester: Manchester University Press.

Cockett, R. (1995) *Thinking the Unthinkable*. London: Fontana.

Cole, G.D.H. (1950) *Socialist Economics*. London: Victor Gollancz.

Collins, P. (2001) A story of justice, *Prospect*, May: 28–33.

Collins, P. (2003) Inspiring moderation, *Prospect*, September: 10–11.

Commission on Social Justice (1994) *Social Justice: Strategies for National Renewal*. London: Vantage.

Connelly, M. (2004) *We Can Take It!* Harlow: Pearson.

Conservative and Unionist Central Office (1947) *The Industrial Charter*. London: Conservative and Unionist Central Office.

Conservative and Unionist Central Office (1949) *The Right Road for Britain*. London: Conservative and Unionist Central Office.

Conservative and Unionist Central Office (1950) *This Is The Road, the Conservative and Unionist Party's Policy for the General Election 1950*. London: Conservative and Unionist Central Office.

Conservative Central Office (1992) *The Best Future for Britain: the Conservative Manifesto 1992*. London: Conservative Central Office.

Conservative Central Office (1997) *You Can Only Be Sure with the Conservatives: the Conservative Manifesto 1997*. London: Conservative Central Office.

Conservative Party (1970) *A Better Tomorrow: the Conservative Party General Election Manifesto 1970*. London: Conservative Party.

Conservative Party (1979) *The Conservative Manifesto 1979*. London: Conservative Central Office.

Conservative Party (1987) *The Next Moves Forward: the Conservative Manifesto 1987*. London: Conservative Central Office.

Cowley, P. (2005) *The Rebels: How Blair Mislaid His Majority*. London: Politico's.

Crewe, I. and King, A. (1997) *SDP: the Birth, Life and Death of a Party*. Oxford: Oxford University Press.

Cronin, J.E. (2004) *New Labour's Pasts*. Harlow: Pearson.

Crosland, C.A.R. (1956) *The Future of Socialism*. London: Jonathan Cape.

Crosland, C.A.R. (1962) *The Conservative Enemy*. London: Jonathan Cape.

Crossman, R.H.S. (ed.) (1952) *New Fabian Essays*. London: Turnstile.

Dale, I. (ed.) (2000a) *Conservative Party General Election Manifestos, 1900–1997*. London: Routledge.

Dale, I. (ed.) (2000b) *Labour Party General Election Manifestos, 1900–1997*. London: Routledge.

Davidson, P. (ed.) (2001) *Orwell and Politics*. London: Penguin.

Deacon, A. (2000) Learning from the US? The influence of American ideas upon 'new labour' thinking on welfare reform, *Policy and Politics*, 28(1): 5–18.

Deacon, A. (2002) *Perspectives on Welfare*. Buckingham: Open University Press.

Deakin, N. (1994) *The Politics of Welfare*. Hemel Hempstead: Harvester Wheatsheaf.

Dell, E. (1999) *A Strange Eventful History: Democratic Socialism in Britain*. London: HarperCollins.

Denham, A. and Garnett, M. (2001) From 'Guru' to 'Godfather': Keith Joseph, 'New' Labour and the British Conservative tradition, *Political Quarterly*, 72(1): 97–106.

Department for Education and Employment (1999) *Excellence in Cities*. London: Stationery Office.

Department of Social Security (1997) *Households Below Average Incomes*. London: Stationery Office.

Department of Social Security (2001) *Households Below Average Incomes*. London: Stationery Office.

Diamond, P. (ed.) (2004) *New Labour's Old Roots*. Exeter: Imprint.

Digby, A. (1989) *British Workhouse Policy: Workhouse to Workfare*. London: Faber & Faber.

Donoughue, B. (2003) *The Heat of the Kitchen*. London: Politico's.

Donoughue, B. and Jones, G.W. (2001) *Herbert Morrison*. London: Phoenix.

Dorey, P. (1995) *British Politics Since 1945*. Oxford: Blackwell.

Dorey, P. (2002) Industrial relations as 'human relations': Conservatism and trade unionism, 1945–64, in S. Ball and I. Holliday (eds) *Mass Conservatism: the Conservatives and the Public Since the 1880s*. London: Frank Cass: 139–62.

Driver, S. (2004) North Atlantic drift: welfare reform and the 'third way' politics of New Labour and the New Democrats, in S. Hale, W. Leggett and L. Martell (eds) *The Third Way and Beyond*. Manchester: Manchester University Press, 31–47.

Driver, S. and Martell, L. (2006) *New Labour*, 2nd edn. Cambridge: Polity.

Durbin, E.F.M. (1940) *The Politics of Democratic Socialism*. London: Routledge & Sons.

Dutton, D. (1991) *British Politics Since 1945: the Rise and Fall of Consensus*. Oxford: Blackwell.

Ellison, N. (1994) *Egalitarian Thought and Labour Politics*. London: Routledge.

Enthoven, A. (1985) *Reflections on the Management of the NHS*. London: National Provincial Trusts.

Esping-Andersen, G. (1990) *The Three Worlds of Welfare Capitalism*. London: Sage.

Etzioni, A. (1997) *The New Golden Rule*. New York: Basic.

Evans, E.J. (2004) *Thatcher and Thatcherism*, 2nd edn. London: Routledge.

Fielding, S. (ed) (1997) *The Labour Party 'Socialism' and Society Since 1951*. Manchester: Manchester University Press.

Fielding, S. (2003a) *The Labour Party*. Basingstoke: Palgrave Macmillan.

Fielding, S. (2003b) *The Labour Governments 1964–1970. Volume 1: Labour and Cultural Change*. Manchester: Manchester University Press.

Fielding, S., Thompson, P. and Tiratsoo, N. (1995) *'England Arise!' The Labour Party and Popular Politics in 1940s Britain*. Manchester: Manchester University Press.

Finlayson, A. (2003) *Making Sense of New Labour*. London: Lawrence & Wishart.

Foot, P. (1965) *Immigration and Race in British Politics*. Harmondsworth: Penguin.

Fowler, N. (1991) *Ministers Decide*. London: Chapmans.

Francis, M. (1997) *Ideas and Policies Under Labour 1945–1951*. Manchester: Manchester University Press.

Francis, M. (2000) Labour and gender, in D. Tanner, P. Thane and N. Tiratsoo (eds) *Labour's First Century*. Cambridge: Cambridge University Press: 191–220.

Fraser, D. (1973) *The Evolution of the British Welfare State*. London: Macmillan.

Freeden, M. (1999) The ideology of New Labour, *Political Quarterly*, 70(1): 42–51.

Gamble, A. (1988) *The Free Economy and the Strong State*. Basingstoke: Macmillan.

Gamble, A. and Wright, T. (1999) Introduction: the new Social Democracy, in A. Gamble and T. Wright (eds) *The New Social Democracy*. Oxford: Blackwell, 1–9.

Gardiner, J. (2004) *Wartime: Britain 1939–1945*. London: Headline.

Garnett, M. (2003) A question of definition? Ideology and the Conservative Party, 1997–2001, in M. Garnett and P. Lynch (eds) *The Conservatives in Crisis*. Manchester: Manchester University Press: 107–24.

Garnett, M. (2006) *Principles and Politics in Contemporary Britain*, 2nd edn. Exeter: Imprint Academic.

George, V. (1973) *Social Security and Society*. London: Routledge & Kegan Paul.

George, V. and Wilding, P. (1976) *Ideology and Social Welfare*. London: Routledge & Kegan Paul.

Giddens, A. (1994) *Beyond Left and Right*. Cambridge: Polity.

Giddens, A. (1998) *The Third Way*. Cambridge: Polity.

Giddens, A. (2000) *The Third Way and Its Critics*. Cambridge: Polity.

Giddens, A. (2002) *Where Now for New Labour?* Cambridge: Polity.

Gilbert, B.B. (1970) *British Social Policy 1914–1939*. London: Batsford.

Gillman, P. and Gillman, L. (1980) *'Collar the Lot!': How Britain Interned and Expelled its Wartime Refugees*. London: Quartet.

Gilmour, I. (1992) *Dancing with Dogma*. London: Simon & Schuster.

Gilmour, I. and Garnett, M. (1998) *Whatever Happened to the Tories*. London: Fourth Estate.

Ginsburg, N. (2005) The privatization of council housing, *Critical Social Policy*, 25(1): 115–35.

Gladstone, D. (1999) *The Twentieth-Century Welfare State*. Basingstoke: Macmillan.

Gladstone, D. (2003) History and social policy, in P. Alcock, A. Erskine and M. May (eds) *The Student's Companion to Social Policy*. Oxford: Blackwell, 25–30.

Glennerster, H. (2005) The health and welfare legacy, in A. Seldon and D. Kavanagh (eds) *The Blair Effect 2001–5*. Cambridge: Cambridge University Press: 283–305.

Glennerster, H. (2007) *British Social Policy 1945 to the Present*, 3rd edn. Oxford: Blackwell.

Glennerster, H. and Hills, J. (eds) (1998) *The State of Welfare*, 2nd edn. Oxford: Oxford University Press.

Glynn, S. (1999) Employment, in R. M. Page and R. Silburn, (eds) *British Social Welfare in the Twentieth Century*. Basingstoke: Macmillan: 179–98.

Gould, P. (1998) *The Unfinished Revolution*. London: Little, Brown & Co.

Green, D.G. and Lucas, D. (1992) Private welfare in the 1980s, in N. Manning and R. Page (eds) *Social Policy Review 4*. Canterbury: Social Policy Association: chapter 3.

Green, E.H.H. (2002) *Ideologies of Conservatism*. Oxford: Oxford University Press.

Green, E.H.H. (2006) *Thatcher*. London: Hodder Arnold.

Gregg, P. and Harness, S. (2003) Welfare reform and the employment of lone parents in R. Dickens, P. Gregg and J. Wadsworth (eds) *The Labour Market Under New Labour*. Basingstoke: Palgrave.

Griffiths, J. (1969) *Pages From Memory*. London: Dent.

Griffiths Report (1988) *Community Care: Agenda for Action*. London: HMSO.

Hale, S. (2002) Professor Macmurray and Mr Blair: the strange case of the communitarian guru that never was, *Political Quarterly*, 73(2): 191–7.

Hall, S. (1998) The great moving nowhere show, *Marxism Today*, Special Issue, Nov/Dec: 9–14.

Hall, S. (2003) New Labour has picked up where Thatcherism left off, *The Guardian*, 2 August 2003.

Halpern, D., Bates, C., Mulgan, G., Aldridge, S., Beales, G. and Heathfield, A. (2004) *Personal Responsibility and Changing Behaviour: the State of Knowledge and its Implications for Public Policy*. London: Cabinet Office.

Ham, C. (1999) *Health Policy in Britain*, 4th edn. Basingstoke: Macmillan.

Harker, L. (2005) A 21st century welfare state, in N. Pearce and W. Paxton (eds) *Social Justice: Building a Fairer Britain*. London: Politico's, 263–81.

Harmer, H. (1999) *The Labour Party 1900–1998*. London: Longman.

Harris, B. (2004) *The Origins of the British Welfare State: Society, State and Social Welfare in England and Wales, 1800–1945*. Basingstoke: Palgrave Macmillan.

Harris, J. (1997) *William Beveridge: a Biography*. Rev edn. Oxford: Clarendon.

Harris, J. (2000) Labour's political and social thought, in D. Tanner, P. Thane and N. Tirtatsoo (eds) *Labour's First Century*. Cambridge: Cambridge University Press, 8–45.

Harrison, B. (2004) Joseph, Keith Sinjohn, Baron Joseph (1918–1994) *Oxford Dictionary of National Biography*. Oxford: Oxford University Press. Available at: http://www.oxforddnb.com/view/article/55063 (accessed 3 November 2006).

Harrison, T. (1978) *Living Through the Blitz*. Harmondsworth: Penguin.

Harrop, M. and Scammell, M. (1992) A tabloid war, in D. Butler and D. Kavanagh (eds) *The British General Election of 1992*. Basingstoke: Macmillan, 180–210.

Hay, C. (1999) *The Political Economy of New Labour: Labouring Under False Pretences?* Manchester: Manchester University Press.

Hay, J.R. (1983) *The Origins of the Liberal Welfare Reforms 1906–14*, Rev edn. London: Macmillan.

Hayek, F.A. (1944) *The Road to Serfdom*. London: Routledge.

Heffernan, R. (2000) *New Labour and Thatcherism*. Basingstoke: Palgrave.

Heffernan, R. (2002) The possible as the art of politics understanding consensus politics, *Political Studies*, 50(4): 742–60.

Hennessy, P. (1993) *Never Again: Britain 1945–1951*. London: Vintage.

Hickson, K. (2004a) The postwar consensus revisited, *Political Quarterly*, 14(2): 142–54.

Hickson, K. (2004b) Economic thought, in A. Seldon and K. Hickson (eds) *New Labour, Old Labour: the Wilson and Callaghan Governments, 1974–79*. London: Routledge, 34–51.

Hickson, K. (ed) (2005) *The Political Thoughts of the Conservative Party Since 1945*. Basingstoke: Palgrave Macmillan.

Hill, M. (1993) *The Welfare State in Britain*. Aldershot: Edward Elgar.

Hills, J. (1993) *The Future of Welfare: a Guide to the Debate*. York: Joseph Rowntree Foundation.

Hills, J. (1998) Housing: a decent home within the reach of every family? in H. Glennerster and J. Hills (eds) *The State of Welfare*, 2nd edn. Oxford: Oxford University Press, 122–88.

Hills, J. (2001) Poverty and social security: what rights? Whose responsibilities, in A. Park, J. Curtice, K. Thomson, L. Jarvis, and C. Bromley (eds) *British Social Attitudes: the 18th Report*. London: Sage, chapter 1.

Hills, J. and Stewart, K. (eds) (2005a) *A More Equal Society? New Labour, Poverty, Inequality and Exclusion*. Bristol: Policy.

Hills, J. and Stewart, K. (2005b) A tide turned but mountains yet to climb in J. Hills and K. Stewart (eds) *A More Equal Society? New Labour, Poverty, Inequality and Exclusion*. Bristol: Policy, 325–46.

Hogg, Q. (1947) *The Case for Conservatism*. Harmondsworth: Penguin.

Holland, S. (1975) *The Socialist Challenge*. London: Quartet.

Howard, N. (2005) *A New Dawn: the General Election of 1945*. London: Politico's.

Howe, G. (1990) Resignation statement, 13 November 1990, *Parliamentary Debates*, 180: cols. 461–5.

Howe, G., Lord (2006) Can 364 economists all be wrong?, in H. Davies (ed.) *The Chancellors' Tales*. Cambridge: Polity, 76–112.

Howell, D. (1976) *British Social Democracy*. London: Croom Helm.

Huntington, N. and Bale, T. (2002) New Labour: new Christian Democracy? *Political Quarterly*, 73(1): 44–50.

Hutton, W. (1994) *The State We're In*. London: Jonathan Cape.

Hylton, S. (2001) *Their Darkest Hour*. Stroud: Sutton.

Jackson, K. (2004) *Humphrey Jennings*. London: Picador.

Jaenicke, D. (2000) New Labour and the Clinton Presidency, in D. Coates and P. Lawler (eds) *New Labour in Power*. Manchester: Manchester University Press, 34–48.

Jay, D. (1937) *The Socialist Case*. London: Faber & Faber.

Jefferys, K. (1992) *The Attlee Governments 1945–1951*. London: Longman.

Jefferys, K. (1997) *Retreat from New Jerusalem*. Basingstoke: Macmillan.

Jefferys, K. (2002) *Finest & Darkest Hours*. London: Atlantic.

Jefferys, K. (ed.) (1994) *War and Reform: British Politics During the Second World War*. Manchester: Manchester University Press.

Jenkins, S. (2006) *Thatcher and Sons*. London: Allen Lane.

Johnson, C. and Tonkiss, F. (2002), The third influence: the Blair government and Australian Labor, *Policy and Politics*, 30(1): 5–18.

Jones, H. (ed.) (1997) *Towards a Classless Society*. London: Routledge.

Jones, H. (1999) Health, in R. M. Page and R. Silburn (eds) *British Social Welfare in the Twentieth Century*. Basingstoke: Macmillan, 159–78.

Jones, H. (2000) 'This is magnificent!': 300,000 houses a year and the Tory revival after 1945, *Contemporary British History*, 14(1): 99–121.

Jones, H. and Kandiah, M. (eds) (1996) *The Myth of Consensus*. Basingstoke: Macmillan.

Jones, M. and Lowe, R. (2002) *From Beveridge to Blair*. Manchester: Manchester University Press.

Jones, T. (1996) *Remaking the Labour Party: from Gaitskell to Blair*. London: Routledge.

Joseph, K. (1959) The social services, in One Nation Group (eds) *The Responsible Society*. London: Conservative Political Centre, 31–41.

Kandiah, M. (1995) The Conservative Party and the 1945 General Election, *Contemporary Record*, 9(1): 22–47.

Kandiah, M. (1996) Conservative leaders, strategy – and 'consensus'? 1945–1964, in H. Jones and M. Kandiah (eds) *The Myth of Consensus*. Basingstoke: Macmillan, 58–78.

Kavanagh, D. (1992) The postwar consensus, *Twentieth Century British History*, 3(2): 175–90.

Kavanagh, D. (1994) A Major agenda? in D. Kavanagh and A. Seldon (eds) *The Major Effect*. London: Macmillan, 3–17.

Kavanagh, D. and Morris, P. (1994) *Consensus Politics from Attlee to Major*, 2nd edn. Oxford: Blackwell.

Kavanagh, D. and Seldon, A. (eds) (1994) *The Major Effect*. London: Macmillan.

Keegan, W. (2003) *The Prudence of Mr Gordon Brown*. Chichester: Wiley.

Kellner, P. (2003) Why ideology is not the answer, *Fabian Review*, 115(4), Winter, 10–11.

Kelly, S. (2002) *The Myth of Mr Butskell: the Politics of British Economic Policy, 1950–55*. Aldershot: Ashgate.

Kent, J. (1992) *William Temple*. Cambridge: Cambridge University Press.

Kincaid, J.C. (1975) *Poverty and Equality in Britain*, Rev. edn. Harmondsworth: Penguin.

King, A.D. and Wickham-Jones, M. (1999) Bridging the Atlantic: the Democratic (Party) origins of welfare to work, in M. Powell (ed.) *New Labour, New Welfare State*. Bristol: Policy, 257–80.

Kinnock, N. (2000) New? We've always been new, *New Statesman*, 28 February 2000: 28.

Klein, R. (1995) *The New Politics of the NHS*, 3rd edn. London: Longman.

Kramnick, I. and Sheerman, B. (1993) *Harold Laski: a Life on the Left*. London: Hamish Hamilton.

Kushner, T. (1989) *The Persistence of Prejudice*. Manchester: Manchester University Press.

Labour Party (1945) *Let Us Face The Future: a Declaration of Labour Policy for the Consideration of the Nation.* London: Labour Party.

Labour Party (1950) *Let Us Win Through Together: a Declaration of Labour Policy for the Consideration of the Nation.* London: Labour Party.

Labour Party (1951a) *Labour Party Election Manifesto.* London: Labour Party.

Labour Party (1951b) *A Policy for Secondary Education.* London: Labour Party.

Labour Party (1960) *Labour in the Sixties.* London: Labour Party.

Labour Party (1961) *Signposts for the Sixties.* London: Labour Party.

Labour Party (1964) *Let's Go With Labour for the New Britain. The Labour Party's Manifesto for the 1964 General Election.* London: Labour Party.

Labour Party (1974) *The Labour Party Manifesto 1974. Let Us Work Together – Labour's Way Out of the Crisis.* London: Labour Party.

Labour Party (1997) *New Labour Because Britain Deserves Better. The Labour Party Manifesto for the 1997 General Election.* London: Labour Party.

Labour Party (2001) *Ambitions for Britain. The Labour Party Manifesto for the 2001 General Election.* London: Labour Party.

Labour Party (2005) *Britain forward not back. The Labour Party Manifesto for the 2005 General Election.* London: Labour Party.

Lafitte, F. (1944) *The Internment of Aliens.* London: Penguin.

Law, R. (1950) *Return from Utopia.* London: Faber.

Lawson, N. (1992) *The View from No 11: Memoirs of a Tory Radical.* London: Bantam.

Lawson, N. (2005) *Dare More Democracy.* London: Compass.

Le Grand, J. (1999) Conceptions of social justice, in R. Walker (ed.) *Ending Child Welfare: Popular Welfare for the 21st Century?* Bristol: Policy, 65–7.

Le Grand, J. (2003) *Motivation, Agency and Public Policy.* Oxford: Oxford University Press.

Le Grand, J. (2005) Inequality, choice and public services, in A. Giddens and P. Diamond (eds) *The New Egalitarianism.* Cambridge: Polity, 200–10.

Lees, D.S. (1961) *Health Through Choice.* London: Institute of Economic Affairs.

Leggett, W. (2004) Social change, values and political agency: the case of the third way, *Politics*, 24(1): 12–19.

Leggett, W. (2005) *After New Labour: Social Theory and Centre Left Politics.* Basingstoke: Palgrave Macmillan.

Levine, J. (2006) *Forgotten Voices of the Blitz and the Battle for Britain.* London: Edbury.

Levitas, R. (2005) *The Inclusive Society?* 2nd edn. Basingstoke: Palgrave Macmillan.

Lewis, P. (1986) *A People's War.* London: Thames Methuen.

Lipsey, D. (2005) Too much choice, *Prospect*, December: 26–9.

Lowe, R. (1989) Resignation at the Treasury: the Social Services Committee and the failure to reform the welfare state, 1955–57, *Journal of Social Policy*, 18(4): 505–26.

Lowe, R. (1990) The second world war, consensus, and the foundation of the welfare state, *Twentieth Century British History*, 1(2): 152–82.

Lowe, R. (1996) The replanning of the welfare state, 1957–1964, in M. Francis and I. Zweiniger-Bargielowska (eds) *The Conservatives and British Society, 1880–1990.* Cardiff: University of Wales Press, 255–73.

Lowe, R. (2004a) Review of R. Mackay (2002), *Half the Battle*. Manchester: Manchester University Press, in *American Historical Review*, 109(2): 619.

Lowe, R. (2005) *The Welfare State in Britain Since 1945*, 3rd edn. Basingstoke: Palgrave Macmillan.

Lowe, R.A. (2004b) Education policy, in A. Seldon and K. Hickson (eds) *New Labour, Old Labour: the Wilson and Callaghan Governments, 1974–9*. London: Routledge, 123–38.

Ludlam, S. and Smith, M.J. (eds) (2004) *Governing as New Labour*, Basingstoke: Palgrave Macmillan.

Lunn, K. (1993) 'Race' and immigration: Labour's hidden history 1945–51, in J. Fyrth (ed.) *Labour's High Noon: the Government and the Economy 1945–51*. London: Lawrence & Wishart, 227–42.

Mackay, R. (2002) *Half the Battle: Civilian Morale in Britain During the Second World War*. Manchester: Manchester University Press.

Macleod, I. and Maude, A. (eds) (1950) *One Nation. A Tory Approach to Social Problems*. London: Conservative Political Centre.

Macmillan, H. (1938) *The Middle Way*. London: Macmillan.

Major, J. (2000) *John Major: the Autobiography*. London: HarperCollins.

Malpass, P. (2003) The wobbly pillar? Housing and the British postwar welfare state, *Journal of Social Policy*, 32(4): 589–606.

Malpass, P. (2005) *Housing and the Welfare State*. Basingstoke: Palgrave Macmillan.

Mandelson, P. and Liddle, R. (1996) *The Blair Revolution*. London: Faber.

Marquand, D. (1999) Premature obsequies: social democracy comes in from the cold, *Political Quarterly*, 70, special edition: 10–18.

Marquand, D. (2000) History today, *Fabian Review*, 112(1), Spring: 2–3.

Marquand, D. (2004) The Welsh wrecker, in A. Adonis and K. Thomas (eds) *Roy Jenkins a Retrospective*. Oxford: Oxford University Press, 109–38.

Marwick, A. (2003) *British Society Since 1945*. 4th edn. London: Penguin.

Mason, T. and Thompson, P. (1991) Reflections on a revolution? The political mood in wartime Britain, in N. Tiratsoo (ed.) *The Attlee Years*. London: Pinter, 54–70.

May, M. (2001) Women and the 'third way': the implications of work-based welfare, *Critical Social Policy*, 21(4), November: 522–5.

McCarthy, M. (1986) *Campaigning for the Poor: CPAG and the Politics of Welfare*. London: Croom Helm.

McCullum, R.B. and Readman, A. (1964) *The British General Election of 1945*. London: Frank Cass.

McKibbin, R. (1998) *Classes and Cultures: England 1918–1951*. Oxford: Oxford University Press.

McKnight, A. (2005) Employment: tackling poverty through 'work for those who can', in J. Hills and K. Stewart (eds) *A More Equal Society? New Labour, Poverty, Inequality and Exclusion*. Bristol: Policy, 23–46.

McKnight, A., Glennerster, H. and Lupton, R. (2005) Education, education, education . . .: an assessment of Labour's success in tackling education inequalities, in J. Hills and K. Stewart (eds) *A More Equal Society? New Labour, Poverty, Inequality and Exclusion*. Bristol: Policy, 47–68.

McLaine, I. (1979) *Ministry of Morale*. London: Allen & Unwin.

McNicol, J. (1986) The evacuation of school children, in H. L. Smith (ed.) *War and Social Change*. Manchester: Manchester University Press, 3–31.

Miliband, R. (1961) *Parliamentary Socialism*. London: Allen & Unwin.

Milne, S. (2004) *The Enemy Within*, 3rd edn. London: Verso.

Mishra, R. (1977) *Society and Social Policy*. London: Macmillan.

Morgan, K.O. (1984) *Labour in Power 1945–1951*. Oxford: Clarendon.

Morgan, K.O. (1992) *The People's Peace*. Oxford: Oxford University Press.

Morgan, K.O. (2004) The judgement of history, *The Independent on Sunday*, 25 January 2004.

Mosley, L. (1974) *Backs to the Wall*. London: Book Club Associates.

Mulgan, G. (2005) Going with and against the grain: social policy in practice since 1997, in N. Pearce and W. Paxton (eds) *Social Justice: Building a Fairer Britain*. London: Politico's, 88–105.

Murray, C. (1980) *Losing Ground*. New York: Basic.

National Council of Inquiry into Higher Education (1997) *Higher Education in the Learning Society*, The Dearing Report. London: HMSO.

Nissan, D. and Le Grand, J. (2003) *A Capital Idea: Start-Up Grants for Young People*. London: Fabian Society.

No Turning Back Group (1993) *Who Benefits? Reinventing Social Security*. London: No Turning Back Group.

O'Connor, J. (1973) *The Fiscal Crisis of the State*. New York: St Martin's Press.

O'Hara, K. (2007) *After Blair: David Cameron and the Conservative Tradition*. London: Icon.

One Nation Group (1959) *The Responsible Society*. London: Conservative Political Centre.

Page, R.M. (1984) *Stigma*. London: Routledge & Kegan Paul.

Page, R.M. (1995) The attack on the British welfare state – more real than imagined? A leveller's tale, *Critical Social Policy*, 44/45, Autumn: 220–28.

Page, R.M. (1997) Young single mothers, in H. Jones (ed.) *Towards a Classless Society*. London: Routledge, 151–78.

Page, R.M. (2007) Without a song in their heart: New Labour, the welfare state and the retreat from democratic socialism, *Journal of Social Policy*, 36(1): 19–37.

Palmer, G., North, J., Carr, J. and Kenway, P. (2003) *Monitoring Poverty and Social Exclusion 2003*. York: Joseph Rowntree Foundation.

Palmer, G., MacInnes, T. and Kenway, P. (2006) *Monitoring Poverty and Social Exclusion 2006*. York: Joseph Rowntree Foundation.

Park, A., Curtice, J., Thomson, K., Jarvis, L. and Bromley, C. (eds) (2003), *British Social Attitudes, the 20th Report*. London: Sage.

Peacock, A. and Wiseman, J. (1964) *Education for Democrats: a Study of the Financing of Education in a Free Society*. London: Institute of Economic Affairs.

Pearce, N. and Paxton, W. (eds) (2005) *Social Justice: Building a Fairer Britain*. London: Politico's.

Pearce, R. (1994) *Attlee's Labour Governments 1945–51*. London: Routledge.

Pearce, R. (1997) *Attlee*. London: Longman.

Piachaud, D. (2001) Child poverty, opportunities and quality of life, *Political Quarterly*, 21(4): 446–53.

Pierson, C. (2001) *Hard Choices*. Cambridge: Polity.

Pierson, C. and Castles, F.G. (2002) Australian antecedents of the third way, *Political Studies*, 50(4): 683–702.

Pimlott, B. (1985) *Hugh Dalton*. London: Jonathan Cape.

Pimlott, B. (1988) The myth of consensus, in L.M. Smith (ed.) *The Making of Britain: Echoes of Greatness*. Basingstoke: Macmillan, 129–141.

Pimlott, B. (1992) *Harold Wilson*. London: HarperCollins.

Plant, R. (2002) Tony Crosland, in K. Jefferys (ed.) *Labour Forces*. London: I.B. Tauris, 119–33.

Plant, R. (2004) Ends, means and political identity, in R. Plant, M. Beech and K. Hickson (eds) *The Struggle for Labour's Soul*. London: Routledge, 105–19.

Plant, R., Beech, M. and Hickson, K. (eds) (2004) *The Struggle for Labour's Soul*. London: Routledge.

Pollitt, C. (1993) *Managerialism and the Public Services*, 2nd edn. Oxford: Blackwell.

Pollock, A.M. (2004) *NHS plc*. London: Verso.

Powell, E. and Maude, A. (eds) (1954) *Change is our Ally*. London: Conservative Political Centre.

Powell, M. (2002) Introduction, in M. Powell (ed.) *Evaluating New Labour's Welfare Reforms*. Bristol: Policy, 1–17.

Prideaux, S. (2005) *Not So New Labour*. Bristol: Policy.

Priestley, J.B. (1940) *Postscripts*. London: Heinemann.

Purdy, D. (2000) New Labour and welfare reform, in D. Coates and P. Lawler (eds) *New Labour in Power*. Manchester: Manchester University Press, 181–94.

Raison, T. (1990) *Tories and the Welfare State*. Basingstoke: Macmillan.

Randall, N. (2004) Three faces of New Labour: principle, pragmatism and populism in New Labour's Home Office, in S. Ludlam and M. J. Smith (eds) *Governing As New Labour*. Basingstoke: Palgrave Macmillan, 177–92.

Reisman, D.A. (1977) *Richard Titmuss: Welfare and Society*. London: Heinemann.

Report on an Inquiry into the Accident at Bethnal Green Tube Station Shelter (1945). London: HMSO.

Richards, P. (ed.) (2004) *Tony Blair in His Own Words*. London: Politico's.

Ridley, N. (1991) *'My Style of Government', The Thatcher Years*. London: Hutchinson.

Ritschel, D. (1995) Macmillan, in V. George and R. Page (eds) *Modern Thinkers on Welfare*. Hemel Hempstead: Prentice-Hall/Harvester Wheatsheaf.

Rollings, N. (1996) Butskellism, the postwar consensus and the managed economy, in H. Jones and M. Kandiah (eds) *The Myth of Consensus*. Basingstoke: Macmillan, 97–119.

Rubinstein, D. (1997) How new is New Labour? *Political Quarterly*, 68(4): 339–43.

Rubinstein, D. (2000) A new look at New Labour, *Politics*, 20(3): 161–7.

Rubinstein, W.D. (2003) *Twentieth-Century British History*. Basingstoke: Palgrave.

Sandbrook, D. (2005) *Never Had It So Good*. London: Little, Brown and Co.

Sandbrook, D. (2006) *White Heat*. London: Little, Brown and Co.

Sassoon, D. (1997) *One Hundred Years of Socialism*. London: HarperCollins.

Saville, J. (1977) The welfare state: an historical approach, in M. Fitzgerald, P. Halmos, J. Muncie and D. Zeldin (eds) *Welfare in Action*. London: Routledge & Kegan Paul, 4–9.

Schwartz, B. (2005) *The Paradox of Choice*. London: Ecco.

Searle, G.R. (2001) *The Liberal Party*. Basingstoke: Palgrave.

Seawright, D. (2005) One Nation, in K. Hickson (ed.) *The Political Thought of the Conservative Party Since 1945*. Basingstoke: Palgrave Macmillan, 69–90.

Sefton, T. (2003) What we want from the welfare state, in A. Park, J. Curtice. K. Thomson, L. Jarvis and C. Bromley (eds) *British Social Attitudes: the 20th Report*. London: Sage, 1–28.

Seldon, A. (1981) *Churchill's Indian Summer*. London: Hodder & Stoughton.

Seldon, A. (1994) Consensus: a debate too long? *Parliamentary Affairs*, 47(4): 501–14.

Seldon, A. and Hickson, K. (eds) (2004a) *New Labour, Old Labour: the Wilson and Callaghan Governments, 1974–7*. London: Routledge.

Seldon, A. and Hickson, K. (2004b) Introduction, in A. Seldon and K. Hickson (eds) *New Labour, Old Labour: the Wilson and Callaghan Governments. 1974–79*. London: Routledge, 1–2.

Seldon, A. and Kavanagh, D. (eds) (2005) *The Blair Effect 2001–5*. Cambridge: Cambridge University Press.

Seldon, A.F. (1957) *Pensions in a Free Society*. London: Institute of Economic Affairs.

Shaw, E. (1996) *The Labour Party Since 1945*. Oxford: Blackwell.

Shepherd, R. (1996) *Enoch Powell*. London: Pimlico.

Smith, H.L. (ed.) (1986) *War and Social Change*. Manchester: Manchester University Press.

Smith, H.L. (ed.) (1996) *Britain in the Second World War: A Social History*. Manchester: Manchester University Press.

Smith, M. (2000) *Britain and 1940*. London: Routledge.

Smith, M.J. (2004) Conclusion: defining New Labour, in S. Ludlam and M.J. Smith (eds) *Governing as New Labour*. Basingstoke: Palgrave Macmillan, 210–25.

Smithers, A. (2005) Education, in A. Seldon and D. Kavanagh (eds) *The Blair Effect 2001–5*. Cambridge: Cambridge University Press, 256–82.

Smithies, E. (1982) *Crime in Wartime: a Social History of Crime in World War II*. London: Allen & Unwin.

Stewart, J. (1999) *The Battle in Health: a Political History of the Socialist Medical Association*. Aldershot: Ashgate.

Stewart, K. (2005) Towards an equal start? Addressing childhood poverty and deprivation, in J. Hills and K. Stewart (eds) *A More Equal Society? New Labour, Poverty, Inequality and Exclusion*. Bristol: Policy, 143–65.

Sullivan, M. (1992) *The Politics of Social Policy*. Hemel Hempstead: Harvester Wheatsheaf.

Summerfield, P. (1981) Education and politics in the British armed forces in the second world war, *International Review of Social History*, xxxvi(2): 133–58.

Sutherland, H., Sefton, T. and Piachaud, D. (2003) *Poverty in Britain: the Impact of Government Policy Since 1997*. York: Joseph Rowntree Foundation.

Taylor, A. (2002) Speaking to democracy: the Conservative Party and mass opinion from the 1920s to the 1950s, in S. Ball and I. Holliday (eds) *Mass Conservatism: the Conservatives and the Public Since the 1880s*. London: Frank Cass, 78–99.

Taylor-Gooby, P. (2000) Blair's scars, *Critical Social Policy*, 20(3): 331–48.

Taylor-Gooby, P., Larsen, T. and Kananen, J. (2004) Market means and welfare ends: the UK welfare state experiment, *Journal of Social Policy*, 33(4): 573–92.

Temple, W. (1942) *Christianity and the Social Order*. London: Penguin.

Thatcher, M. (1995) *The Path to Power*. London: HarperCollins.

Thomas, D. (2003) *An Underworld at War*. London: John Murray.

Thompson, N. (1996) *Political Economy and the Labour Party*. London: UCL.

Thorpe, A. (2001) *A History of the British Labour Party*, 2nd edn. Basingstoke: Palgrave.

Timmins, N. (2001) *The Five Giants*, rev. and updated edn. London: HarperCollins.

Tiratsoo, N. (ed.) (1995) *From Blitz to Blair*. London: Weidenfeld & Nicolson.

Titmuss, R.M. (1950) *Problems of Social Policy*. London: HMSO and Longmans, Green & Co.

Titmuss, R.M. (1970) *The Gift Relationship*. London: Allen & Unwin.

Tomlinson, J. (1992) Planning: debate and policy in the 1940s, *Twentieth Century British History*, 3(2): 154–74.

Tomlinson, J. (1997a) *Democratic Socialism and Economic Policy: the Attlee Years 1945–1951*. Cambridge: Cambridge University Press.

Tomlinson, J. (1997b) Reconstructing Britain: Labour in power 1945–1951, in N. Tiratsoo (ed.) *From Blitz to Blair*. London: Weidenfeld & Nicolson, 77–101.

Tomlinson, J. (1998) Why so austere? The British welfare state of the 1940s, *Journal of Social Policy*, 27(1): 63–77.

Tomlinson, J. (2000) Labour and the economy, in D. Tanner, P. Thane and N. Tiratsoo (eds) *Labour's First Century*. Cambridge: Cambridge University Press, 46–79.

Tomlinson, J. (2004a) *The Labour Governments 1964–1970, Volume 3, Economic Policy*. Manchester: Manchester University Press.

Tomlinson, J. (2004b) Economic policy, in A. Seldon and K. Hickson (eds) *New Labour, Old Labour: the Wilson and Callaghan Governments. 1974–79*. London: Routledge, 55–69.

Townsend, P. (1958) A society for people, in N. Mackenzie (ed.) *Conviction*. London: MacGibbon & Kee, 93–120.

Townsend, P. (1995) Persuasion and conformity: an assessment of the Borrie Report on Social Justice, *New Left Review*, 213, September/October: 137–50.

Toynbee, P. and Walker, D. (2001) *Did Things Get Better?* Harmondsworth: Penguin.

Toynbee, P. and Walker, D. (2004) Social policy and inequality, in A. Seldon and K. Hickson (eds) *New Labour, Old Labour: the Wilson and Callaghan Governments, 1974–9*. London: Routledge, 105–22.

Toynbee, P. and Walker, D. (2005), *Better or Worse? Has Labour Delivered?* London: Bloomsbury.

Travers, T. (2005) Local and central government, in A. Seldon and D. Kavanagh (eds) *The Blair Effect 2001–5*. Cambridge: Cambridge University Press, 68–93.

Turner, J. (1995) A land fit for Tories to live in: the political ecology of the British Conservative Party, 1944–94, *Contemporary European History*, 4(2): 189–208.

Veit-Wilson, J. (2000) States of welfare: a conceptual challenge, *Social Policy and Administration*, 34(1): 1–25.

Waller, M. (2005) *London 1945*. London: John Murray.

Walsha, R. (2000) The One Nation Group: a Tory Approach to backbench politics and organization, 1950–55, *Twentieth Century British History*, 11(2): 183–214.

Walsha, R. (2003) The One Nation Group and One Nation Conservatism, 1950–2002, *Contemporary British History*, 17(2), Summer: 69–120.

Webster, C. (2002) *The National Health Service*, 2nd edn. Oxford: Oxford University Press.

Wetherly, P. (2001) The reform of welfare and the way we live now: a critique of Giddens and the Third Way, *Contemporary Politics*, 7(2): 149–68.

White, S. (2001a) *New Labour: the Progressive Future*. London: Palgrave.

White, S. (2001b) The ambiguities of the Third Way in S. White (ed.) *New Labour: the Progressive Future*. London: Palgrave: 3–17.

Whiteside, N. (1996) The politics of the 'social' and the 'industrial' wage, 1945–60, in H. Jones and M. Kandiah (eds) *The Myth of Consensus*. Basingstoke: Macmillan, 120–38.

Whiting, R. (2000) *The Labour Party and Taxation*. Cambridge: Cambridge University Press.

Wilcox, S. (2002) *UK Housing Review 2002/3*. York: Joseph Rowntree Foundation.

Willetts, D. (1992) *Modern Conservatism*. Harmondsworth: Penguin.

Williams, F. (2001) In and beyond New Labour: towards a new political ethics of care, *Critical Social Policy*, 21(4), November: 467–93.

Willman, J. (1994) The Civil Service, in D. Kavanagh and A. Seldon (eds) *The Major Effect*. London: Macmillan, 64–82.

Wring, D. (2005) *The Politics of Marketing the Labour Party*. Basingstoke: Palgrave Macmillan.

Young, H. (1993) *One of Us*, final edn. London: Pan.

Zweiniger-Bargielowska, I. (1996) Explaining the gender gap: the Conservative Party and the women's vote, 1945–1964, in M. Francis and I. Zweiniger (eds) *The Conservatives and British Society, 1880–1990*. Cardiff: University of Wales Press, 194–223.

Zweiniger-Bargielowska, I. (2000) *Austerity in Britain: Rationing, Controls and Consumption 1939–1955*. Oxford: Oxford University Press.

Index